Septimus Rivington

The History of Tonbridge School from its Foundation in 1553 to the Present Date

Septimus Rivington

The History of Tonbridge School from its Foundation in 1553 to the Present Date

ISBN/EAN: 9783337326692

Printed in Europe, USA, Canada, Australia, Japan

Cover: Foto ©ninafisch / pixelio.de

More available books at **www.hansebooks.com**

TO

THE REV. JAMES IND WELLDON, D.C.L.

This Work is Dedicated

BY THE AUTHOR,

IN GRATEFUL ACKNOWLEDGMENT OF

MANY KINDNESSES RECEIVED,

AND IN TOKEN OF

SINCERE ESTEEM AND RESPECT.

PREFACE

IF good intentions, and an honest endeavour to carry them out, have any claim to disarm criticism, I trust that the many faults and shortcomings of this volume may be pardoned by my readers. It has long been my wish to see an authentic history of the School compiled; and when the old School was pulled down in 1863, I felt that such a work might considerably help to bridge over the gap that was created between those Old Boys who had passed their School days and had their School recollections wrapped up in the old building, and those who only know the School in its present improved state. It has been my aim to give a simple statement of all that is known on undoubted authority of the School in its earlier days. At the risk of appearing dry, I have avoided garnishing my work with anecdotes, or entering into details about the School within the last few years; but have confined myself to giving full information about the Founder, the Governours, the School estates and revenues, the Head Masters, and Old Boys of note. I gladly take this opportunity of thanking the many friends who have so kindly helped me; especially Dr. Welldon, the Rev. Edward Ind Welldon, J. F. Wadmore, Esq., the Rev. P. R. Sandilands, and W. S. W. Vaux, Esq., of the British Museum. If I have managed to place on record a substantial account of the School, aided by illustrations, and at the same time have succeeded in interesting my readers and the Old Boys, I shall be more than compensated for any little trouble that I may have incurred.

SEPTIMUS RIVINGTON.

88, St. James's Street, S.W
   December, 1869

CONTENTS

	PAGE
THE ORIGIN OF THE SCHOOL	1
SIR ANDREW JUDDE	7
SIR THOMAS SMYTHE	18
HENRY FISHER	25
SIR THOMAS WHITE	27
ROBERT HOLMEDON	30
THOMAS LAMPARD	30
LADY MARY BOSWELL	31
MINOR EXHIBITIONS	31
THE SKINNERS' COMPANY	32
THE CHARTER TO SIR ANDREW JUDDE	35
THE SCHOOL REVENUE	42
THE ORIGINAL STATUTES	48
THE ORIGINAL BUILDING	60
THE OLD ROUTINE OF SCHOOL WORK	63
SKINNERS' DAY	67
VISITORS	74
LIST OF THE HEAD MASTERS	76
JOHN PROCTOUR, M.A.	77
SIR ROBERT HEATH	79
FRANCIS THYNNE	82
JOHN STOCKWOOD, M.A.	84

CONTENTS

	PAGE
WILLIAM HATCH, M.A.	93
MICHAEL JENKINS, M.A.	93
THOMAS HORNE, D.D.	94
NICHOLAS GREY, D.D.	97
JOHN GOAD, B.D.	99
CHRISTOPHER WASE, B.D.	103
THOMAS HERBERT, EARL OF PEMBROKE	107
THOMAS ROOTS, M.A.	109
RICHARD SPENCER, M.A.	112
JAMES CAWTHORN, M.A.	116
WILLIAM WOODFALL	119
JOHNSON TOWERS, M.A.	122
LORD WHITWORTH	123
VICESIMUS KNOX, LL.B.	124
SIR ANTHONY HART	124
VICESIMUS KNOX, D.D.	126
EDWARD DANIEL CLARKE, LL.D.	139
JAMES STANIER CLARKE, D.D.	140
CAPTAIN GEORGE CLARKE, R.N.	140
GENERAL DUMOUSTIER	143
SIR WILLIAM SIDNEY SMITH	143
THOMAS KNOX, D.D.	146
THE PRESENT STATUTES	164
JAMES IND WELLDON, D.C.L.	189
E. I. WELLDON, M.A.	190
THE TERCENTENARY	190
THE CHAPEL	191
THE NEW BUILDINGS	193
THE CRICKET PAVILION	195
LIST OF HEAD BOYS SINCE 1844	195
SCHOLARSHIPS AND EXHIBITIONS	196
SCHOOL LIST IN 1844	197
THE BONFIRE	199
THE BISHOP OF DERRY	201

CONTENTS

	PAGE
THE COMMISSIONERS' REPORT ON THE SCHOOL	202
REPORT BY C. J. ELTON, ESQ.	208
QUESTIONS ADDRESSED TO THE TRUSTEES OF ENDOWED SCHOOLS; WITH THEIR ANSWERS	214
LIST OF DISTINCTIONS GAINED AT THE UNIVERSITIES, ETC.	229
SKINNERS' DAY SPEECHES	233

LIST OF ILLUSTRATIONS

	PAGE
THE SCHOOL FROM 1826 TO 1864, FRONT VIEW (*frontispiece*).	
SIR ANDREW JUDDE'S ARMS	7
SIR ANDREW JUDDE	13
THE SKINNERS' COMPANY'S ARMS	32
THE SCHOOL FROM 1760 TO 1825, FRONT VIEW	60
THE COMMON BOX	64
VICESIMUS KNOX, D.D.	126
INTERIOR OF THE UPPER SCHOOL ABOUT 1835	185
THE SCHOOL FROM 1826 TO 1864, BACK VIEW	187
THE INTERIOR OF THE CHAPEL, LOOKING EAST	193
THE PRESENT SCHOOL, FRONT VIEW	195

THE ORIGIN OF THE SCHOOL

THE origin of the Grammar Schools in England is closely connected with, and in fact forms part of the history of the country during the Middle Ages to the Sixteenth Century. The existence of Schools from an early date of any considerable size is plainly traceable from the time when they were attached to, and formed part of the system of Cathedrals, and were under the direct supervision of the clergy. During the temporary increase of the Religious Houses in the thirteenth century, these Cathedral Schools increased proportionately in number. This increase, however, was but temporary, for during the fourteenth and earlier part of the fifteenth centuries, education, learning, and the study of all literature throughout the country greatly declined[1]. It was chiefly the effect of the disturbances in the east of Europe that soon afterwards gave to literature generally, and classical learning in particular, so strong an impulse that they

Grammar Schools succeeded Religious Houses as a means of education.

---

[1] Hallam, Liter. vol. i. p. 124. Knight's Life of Colet, ed. 1724, p. 14.

never again languished to any thing approaching the extent that they had done during the previous centuries. The taking of Constantinople by the Turks (A.D. 1453) compelled many of the Greeks to fly for protection to Italy and Germany, and from these southern countries they gradually spread west and north, diffusing their knowledge wherever they went [1]. The result of this, together with the invention of printing [2], was to give a sudden and strong impulse for the desire of education in Latin and Greek, generally called the Revival of Learning. The dissolution of the monasteries, also, which supplemented the Cathedrals in their work of education, occasioned a vacuum which was at once felt and provided for by both clergy and laity. The monastic orders had gradually fallen into disrepute, partly owing to the begging orders or Mendicants (particularly the Dominicans and Franciscans) succeeding in the esteem of the world to the place which the monks formerly held [3]. These orders were very ignorant and jealous of the rapid progress of learning; and knew that Erasmus and the other restorers of education looked upon them with contempt, and so they naturally foresaw that the progress of learning was a sign of their eventual downfall [4]. Visitors were appointed to survey the lesser monasteries, with a view to their dissolution and the reorganization of their educational functions. They were required to carry with them the concurrence of the gentry in the neighbourhood, and to examine the state of the revenues and goods of the monasteries. They were to try

Side notes: The desire for education spread from east to west. And Latin and Greek began to be read. Decline of monastic orders. Visitors reported on the lesser monasteries, And took the sense of the sur-

---

[1] Gibbon's Decline and Fall of the Roman Empire, vol. viii. pp. 106, 107. Mosheim, Institut. Hist. Eccles. ed. 1845, vol. ii. pp. 598, 599.
[2] Hegel's Phil. of History, p. 427.
[3] Mosheim, Institut. Hist. Eccles. ed. 1845, vol. ii. pp. 617, 618.
[4] Burnet's Hist. of the Reformation, abridged by Cowie, p. 27.

how many of the religious would take situations and return to a secular course of life; and these reports were to be sent to the Archbishop of Canterbury or the Lord Chancellor[1]. <small>founding inhabitants as to their future disposition.</small>

The Priory[2] which existed at Tonbridge before the foundation of the School was subjected to this visitation, and the feelings of the neighbourhood on the matter are expressed in the answer to the following letter (quoted from the Archæologia Cantiana, 1858, vol. i. p. 31) from the Archbishop of Canterbury to some of the principal inhabitants, proposing either to continue the Priory as a School for the benefit of the surrounding residents, or to erect in its stead a Grammar School for forty boys. <small>Tonbridge Priory. Proposal to supersede it,</small>

"From Archbishop Warham to William Whetual and others, appointing a day for them to certify to him the feelings of the inhabitants for founding a Grammar School at Tunbridge.

'I commende me to you; and where at my late beeing at Tunbridge I required you and other thinhabitants of the same towne and of other places ny adjoynyng, to be here before me this day, to shewe you and their myndes in writing whethir ye and they should think it more expedient to have a free Scole of grammar founded at Tunbridge, for xl scolers, mennys children of those parties, and they afterward to be promoted to Oxford, having exhibition for their fynding at scole there, orelles to have the contynuance of the prioury there, as it hath be used in tymes past: so it is a good multitude of the said towne, according to the said appointment, hath be here with me this present day, shewing as wel by mouthe as by writing, that they think it

---

[1] Burnet's Hist. of the Reformation, abridged by Cowie, p. 151.

[2] Amswick's Hist. of Tunbridge Wells, 1810, p. 105.

more expedient to have the continuation of the said monastery, w^t the priour and his convent, thanne to have a grammar scole; and they have presented a booke of diverse persons names, their neybours, in a grete number, which, as they saith, be of like mynde in that behalve. And considering that ye were to be here this day w^t me in like wise, to make annswer of yor opinion and mynde as this mater, with the names of as many as be of like mynde as ye be of, I gretely marvaile that ye comme not hider to shewe yor annswer therein accordingly. Therefore I requir you to be here w^t me on Monday next, by ix of the clok before noone, to make and ley in yor annswere in this behalve, as ye shal thinke good, w^t the namys of as many other persons as be of yor opinion and mynde in the same mater, to thentent that I may certify my Lord Cardinal thereof accordingly: and yor myndes knowen, I shalbe glad that suche order and wey may be taken in this mater as ye shal thinke may best stand with the pleasire of God and the common weale of thinhabitants of that cuntrey now beeing and which hereafter shalbe: and in case ye can not thus certify me by Monday next, then I requir you to certify me of yor mynde, and of others of like myndes, at Maidestonne, on Sancto Thomas Day next commyng. If ye had made yor annswer herein, I mought have certified my said Lord Cardinal thereof forthw^t, howbeit by yor delay I am compelled to differre the said certificate. At Oxford, the last day of Juny (1525).

Willi^{a}m Cantuar.'

Addressed: to my right welbeloved William Whetual, William Waller and Henry Fane, and to every of theym."

And to found a School in its place.

"From the same to Cardinal Wolsey. The state of feeling among the inhabitants of Tunbridge, at the suppression of the Priory there, and the proposal to found a free school. 'Please it yo' grace to understand, that upon sight of yo' late letter, I wrote immediately to certeyne substantial persons of Tunbrige and thinhabitants to be advertised by theym, what murmur or brute were made then concernyng the prioury there, and if any such were, the same to be diligently suppressed. Whereupon this morenyng I have receved annswere that there is none other rumour or communication there, but only that thinhabitants of that towne, and others ny adjoynying to the same, had levyr to have the said place not suppressed than the contrary, if it might so stand with the kinges Highnes pleasir and yo' graces; whereunto they referreth their desires and myndes in that behalve. Howbeit reaporte is made, that one Henry Fane and one or ij other persons, lately beeing in variance and suyte with the late Priour, wold be glad to have the said priory suppressed, for fere lest if the Priour should be restored, the said plea should contynue. And therefore, as it is sayd, if any rumor be in this mater, it ryseth by the said Henry Fane and his adherents. As toching the parochial priest of Cranebroke, the trouthe is, that his mater was published by hym, to have thadvises of thinhabitants of Cranebroke, by the desire of theym of Tunbrige, bicause this mater concerneth aswel the commoditie of bothe places as the hole cuntrey, and exhibition of their children at scole : and for this consideration they of Tunbrige requirid the myndes and counseile of theym. Wherein they of Cranbroke be of like mynde and desire as they of Tunbrige, submitting theym selfes

The answer was unfavourable to the erection of a School.

therein holely to the kinges graces pleasir and yours. I assure yo' graces that if any suche rumour had be I beeing nigh to such place should have heerd of it from friends. July 3rd. To Lord Cardinal of York and Legate de later.'"

The erection of a School was, therefore, deferred, and nothing more was heard of it till the time of Sir Andrew Judde.

Schools founded about the same time and by the same sort of Founders.
The date of the foundation of the School, the middle of the sixteenth century, was coincident with that of many others of the same kind. Harrow, Rugby, Merchant Taylors', Uppingham, Bedford, Repton, Highgate, and Oakham were founded about the same time and by the same class of persons. Private individuals, well-known citizens or merchants, founded and endowed these Schools, and the efforts of Edward VI. were much aided and imitated on a more liberal scale by private enterprise and benevolence.

Tonbridge School for a long time did not increase in the number of its scholars; and the average of about thirty was maintained till the end of the last century, when Dr. Vicesimus Knox raised the numbers very considerably. Its his-

The history of the School is closely bound up with that of the Head Masters.
tory, if such it can be called, is chiefly connected with its Head Masters, for the records of the Company to whose care it was entrusted contain no information about it of any interest, and the materials which form the basis of this work have been chiefly gathered from a pamphlet published in 1825 by the late Head Master, Dr. Thomas Knox, with considerable additions collected during the last few years from the British Museum and various other sources.

SIR ANDREW JUDDE

SIR ANDREW JUDDE[1], Knight, the founder of Tonbridge School, was born at Tonbridge, but the date of his birth is not known. He was the youngest son of John Judde, Esq., and the nephew twice removed of Archbishop Chichele. An estate between Tonbridge and Tonbridge Wells belonged to his family, which as early as A.D. 1434 was reckoned among the leading gentry of the county of Kent. From this property, which was situated on Quarry Hill and was called "Barden," the family removed to Ashford, near which also they had a seat, memorials of many of them being still in existence in the parish church of that place.

<small>Birth and parentage of the Founder.</small>

<small>His property.</small>

Sir Andrew, when young, went to London, and was apprenticed to the Company of Skinners, a body at that time having considerable eminence in the metropolis as the chief, and, probably, the only traders in skins and furs. It

---

[1] Hasted's History of Kent, vol. ii. pp. 336, 346.

was by means of this trade that Sir Andrew amassed a large fortune, a considerable portion of which he so liberally expended on the foundation of Tonbridge School, just, too, at that period when the need of such and similar institutions was, owing to the Reformation, greatly felt.

Foreign enterprise. The researches of Columbus [1] and of Sebastian Cabot [2], and somewhat later the disastrous but adventurous voyage of Sir Hugh Willoughby [3], had nearly about the same time given an unusual impetus to distant voyages, the chief object of which was the extension of mercantile traffic; while many expeditions to foreign lands, famous alike for the spirit in which they were conceived and for the zeal with which they were carried out, were undertaken by the gallant citizens of London, with the approbation, and sometimes with the active support, of the monarchs then on the English throne.

The trade in skins was very great. Sir Andrew is styled in old documents a "skinner and merchant of Muscovy," the latter being a title which in those days implied that he was a man of importance in the City of London. The trade of which he was one of the representatives was then large and lucrative, owing in some degree to the habit prevailing at Court and among the leading nobility and wealthier classes of wearing furs of the rarest and most valuable kinds. The numerous memoirs in Hakluyt's curious collection of voyages [4] tell us much of the trade with Muscovy, while a glance at the numerous portraits of Englishmen and of Englishwomen during the first half of the sixteenth century exhibits distinctly the universality of the custom of wearing costly furs.

[1] Hakluyt's Voyages, vol. ii. pt. ii.
[2] Biddle's "Memorial of Sebastian Cabot."
[3] Bancroft's "History of America," vol. i. p. 79.
[4] Hakluyt, vol. i. passim.

Besides this, Queen Mary had in 1556 obtained from the then Czar of Russia an exclusive patent for the whole trade to Muscovy, and had thereby secured to the London merchants the substantial benefits arising in those days from a monopoly. It is true that a seafaring life and travels on the continent of Europe were then hazardous in the extreme, the ships employed being rarely fitted either in size or equipment for the tempests they had to encounter, while the inhabitants of the lands were for the most part little better than savages. It should be always remembered that English sailors, traders, and travellers, did far more than the natives of any other nation to promote a civilized intercourse with other lands, while they at the same time exhibited a spirit and an energy in encountering the greatest difficulties and dangers which in the end produced a mighty influence on the position and power of England herself. *Englishmen had the monopoly of the trade to Muscovy. Trading in foreign parts was dangerous, But it had a beneficial effect on the country.*

Reference to the history of England between 1500 and 1560 shows that to this spirit of adventure, aroused throughout the land by the news brought home by these adventurous explorers about the wealth of foreign lands, and by the consequent fitting out of such expeditions as those of Drake and Raleigh, we owe much of the sturdy and unbending resistance of England to the growing pretensions of Spain which culminated in 1584 in the mission of the Armada against us. Sir Andrew Judde himself took part in an expedition of the Merchants' Company, which used to transport their goods to the North of Russia in their own ships; and then, making use of boats shaped from the hollowed trunks of trees, towed them up the River Dwina to Wologda. From Wologda, this merchandise was carried across country by a seven days' journey to Yeraslau, *The Founder went himself to foreign lands, To Russia,* and thence transported down the Wolga to Astrakhan on the shores of the Caspian Sea. In this way, so early as the reign of Edward VI., English goods found their way into Persia and the remoter regions of the East.

Sir Andrew Judde had also visited the African coast and part of Guinea, and had brought home, at Edward VI.'s request[1], some gold dust for the use of the Royal Mint: in fact, as the tablet to his memory says, "To Russia and Muscova, to Spayne and gynny (Guinea) traveld He by land and sea." Hakluyt (vol. ii. pt. ii. p. 330) thus describes an elephant's head he saw kept by Sir Andrew in his house as a memorial of his foreign travels: "This head divers have seen in the house of the worthy merchant, Sir Andrew Judde, where also I saw it and beheld it, not only with my bodily eyes, but more with the eyes of my mind and spirit, considering by the worke, the cunning and the wisdome of the worke-maister: without which consideration, the sight of such strange and wonderfull things may seeme rather curiosities than profitable contemplations."

In 1544 Sir Andrew Judde filled the office of Sheriff of London, and in 1550–1551 was Lord Mayor[2], during which time we have ample testimony from "Proctour's History of Sir Thomas Wyatt's Rebellion" (a copy of which is in

---

[1] Edward VI.'s private journal in the British Museum.

[2] "Somewhat west of this house (Sir Thomas Gresham's), is one other fair house, wherein Sir William Hollis kept his Maioralty, and was buried in the Parish Church of St. Helen. Sir Andrew Jud also kept his Maioralty there, and was buried at St. Helen's. He builded almshouses for six poor Almspeople near to the said Parish Church, and gave lands to the Skinners, out of which they are to give 4s. every week to the six poor almspeople, 8d. the piece, and 25s. 4d. the year in coals amongst them for ever."—Strype's Stow's Survey of London, vol. ii. bk. ii. p. 156.

Dr. Welldon's possession) that Sir Andrew distinguished himself greatly by his loyalty. "Wyat," says he, "and a fewe with him went further as farre as the drawebridge (of Southwark); on the further side whereof he sawe the Lorde Admirall, the Lorde Maiour, Sir Andrew Judde, and one or two other, in consultation, for ordering of the bridge, where unto he gave diligent care a good tyme." These personal exertions in opposing Wyatt's rebellion helped him to gain the favour of Philip of Spain and of Queen Mary; and during his mayoralty, which he kept in a house near St. Helen's Church, Bishopsgate, he displayed great magnificence and hospitality. Sir Andrew was Lord Deputy and Mayor of the Staple[1] of Calais, then in the hands of the English, about 1555; and on Sept. 4, in that year, he received Philip of Spain, who was on his way with a Royal retinue, including the Earls of Arundel, Pembroke, and Huntingdon, to visit the Emperor Charles V. at Brussels. On this occasion, Sir Andrew presented His Majesty with a purse containing a thousand marks in gold, a magnificent gift from a private gentleman of that time. Philip was said to have been so gratified with this reception, that he distributed a thousand crowns to the soldiers at Calais.

And took an active part against Wyatt's rebellion.

Mayor of Calais.

[1] "The merchants of the Staple were the first and most ancient commercial society in England, and were so named from their exporting the staple wares of the kingdom. These staple wares were only the rough materials for manufacture; wool and skins, lead and tin, sheepskins and leather being the chief. The grower of wool contented himself at first with the sale of it at his own door, or at the next town. Hence arose a sort of middle-man, who bought it of him, and begot the traffic between them and the foreign clothmakers, who, from their being established for the sale of their wools in some certain city, commodious for the intercourse, were first named 'Staplars.'"—Gerard Malyne's Centre of Circle of Commerce, Lond. 1623, quoted in Fox Bourne's English Merchants, vol. i. p. 38.

Sir Andrew Judde was of good birth and well-connected on his mother's side; yet it was chiefly by his own personal efforts that he made his fortune and reputation, and acquired the ample wealth of which he made so admirable an use in the foundation and endowment of the School. Fuller, in his "Worthies of England," says, "Sir Andrew Jud, son of John Jud, was born at Tunbridge, in this county, bred a Skinner in London, whereof he became Lord Mayor in 1551 anno. He built Alms houses nigh to St. Ellen's in London, and a stately free School at Tunbridge in Kent, submitting it to the care of the Company of Skinners." His character stood very high as a sound financial agent in positions of trust, in proof of which his name is constantly to be found in the Council Books of Edward VI.'s time, and it is to his credit that "the good Sir Thomas Whyte," the founder of St. John's College, Oxford, "propter eximium amorem in Andream Judde," gave to the school a fellowship belonging to that college[1].

His commercial reputation.

Among the Harleian MSS. in the British Museum is the following curious document relating to a well known historical fact: " A true copy of the counterfeit will, supposed to be the last will and testament of King Edward VI., forged and published under the great seal of England by the confederacy of the Dukes of Suffolk and Northumberland, on behalf of the Lady Jane, eldest daughter of the said Duke of Suffolk, and testified with the hands of 101 chief of the nobility and principal men of this kingdom." Among the signatures is that of Sir Andrew Judde, next in order to Sir Thomas Gresham's. The autographs, of

His signature is appended to the fictitious will of Edward VI.

---

[1] Vide page 27.

course, are not here, as the MS. in the Museum is only a copy of the original.

Sir Andrew Judde died on September 4, 1558, and was buried on the 14th in St. Helen's Church, Bishopsgate, where a small tablet to his memory may be seen, affixed to the wall. On it is a figure of himself kneeling, as represented beneath, with a quaint inscription under it.

SIR ANDREW JUDDE.

Taken from his mural tablet in St. Helen's Church, Bishopsgate.

" To Russia and Muscova,
   To Spayne and gynny withoute fable
Traveld He by land and sea.
   Both Mayre of London and staple,

> The commonwealthe He norished
> So worthelie in all his Daies
> That ech state fywell him loved,
> To his perpetvale prayes.
> Three wyves He had, one was Mary
> Fowre sons one mayde had he by her,
> By Dame Mary had one Dowghtier.
> Thus in the month of September
> A thousand five hundred and fiftey
> And eight, died this worthie staplar
> Worshipynge his posterytye."

The inscription on his tablet.

Machyn in his Diary, p. 174, mentions his funeral as having been conducted with great pomp and ceremony: "The xivth day of September was buried Sir Andrew Jud, skinner, merchant of Muscovy, and late Mayor of London, with a pennon of armes and a x dozen of penselles, skocyons and a herse of wax of v prynse pals garnished with angelles, and poormen in new gownes, and Master Clarenshus (Clarencieux) King of armes, and Master Somersett harold and the morrow masse and a sermon."

His three wives.

His wives were,—

1. Mary, daughter of Sir Thomas Doon, Lord Mayor of London in 1519. By her he had four sons and one daughter. She died in 1550, and her funeral is thus described by Machyn in his Diary (p. 2): "The xixth day of November was buried my Lade Jude, Mayress of London, and wyff of Sir Androu Jude, Mayor of London, and bered in the paryche of Saint Ellen in Byshope gate Stret, for he gayff mony, gownes, and to the powre men of the same citie, amounting to the value of threscore pounds,

The death of his first wife.

Description of her funeral.

three shillings, and eightpence the year, for the which they be bound to pay twelve pounds to the schoole maister and eight pounds to the usher of his free schoole at Tunbridge yearlie for ever."

2. Annys, about whom nothing is known.

3. Mary, heiress of Sir Thomas Mirfen, Lord Mayor of London in 1518, by whom he had one daughter, Alice; from her the family of the late Viscount Strangford is descended. This Alice Judde[1] married Thomas Smythe[2], "Customer," i.e. farmer of the public revenues in the reigns of Queens Mary and Elizabeth, and father of Sir Thomas Smythe.

His two other wives.

Her charitable bequests are thus given by Strype's Stow's "Survey of London," vol. ii. bk. ii. p. 206:—

The charitable bequests of Alice Smith.

"Alice Smith of London, widow, late wife of Thomas

---

[1] The Arundel Society have published a portrait of Alice Judde (No. 213), and also one of Thomas Smythe (No. 221); both are photographs from pictures, the property of the late Viscount Strangford.

[2] A monument remains of Customer Smythe in the Church at Ashford, bearing the following inscription:—

"MEMORIÆ SACRUM.

Hic certâ spe beatæ resurrectionis conditur clarissimus Vir, Thomas Smythe, de Westenhanger Armiger, qui ob spectatam in principem fidem et observantiam dignissimus habebatur, qui portorii vectigalibus in Londini portubus præficeretur, quæ postea triginta millium librarum annuâ pensatione a principe redemit; et singulari in nobiliores liberalitate et amore in mercatores præstitit opes quibus illum Deus Opt. Max. beavit ad Dei gloriam pauperes sublevando, veræ religionis professores fovendo, bonasque literas promovendo et ad reipublicæ usum longinquas navigationes instruendo, novas terras detegendo, et ærarias fodinas aperiendo libens lubensque dedicavit. Jamque annorum plenus cum sexagesimum novum annum implevisset, filiosque sex, sex etiam filias ex Aliciâ charissimâ (sexagenariâ), filiâ et hærede Andrei Judde militis Domini hujus Villæ de Ashford suscepisset, qui in clariores familias matrimonio collocantur, ex hac vitâ firmâ in Christo fide demigravit junii septimo,

Anno Salutis 1591.

Johannes Smythe filius primogenitus, optimo patri matrique charissimæ cæteris filiis filiabus collacrimantibus, ad officiosæ pietatis et posteritatis memoriam moestissimus posuit."

Smith of the same city, Esq., and Customer of the port of London, in her last will and testament bequeathed lands to the value of 15*l*. by the year for ever, to the Company of Skinners, for the augmenting of the pensions of certain poor, inhabiting in eight almshouses, erected by Sir Andrew Jud, Knt., her father, in the parish of Great St. Helen's, Bishopsgate-street, in London. She hath also given in her said last will and testament to other charitable uses, as to hospitals and to the poor of other parishes, and good preachers, the sum of 300*l*. As also to the poor scholars in the two Universities of Oxford and Cambridge the sum of 200*l*. Of which her last will and testament she made her son Thomas Smith, late Sheriff of London, and Richard and Robert Smith her executors. Who have performed the same according to her godly and charitable mind. This paragraph was expressly by Stow himself ordered to be here inserted; whatever the reason was that it happened to be left out in the after-editions."

Sir Andrew's religion.

As to Sir Andrew's religion, it is impossible to say with certainty what it was, but it must be confessed that it is most likely that when the country and the Court were Roman Catholic he was so too, and that when they became Protestant he followed the stream. For the first Head Master[1], he chose a man who was probably half Roman Catholic and half Protestant, for which choice there were no doubt very good reasons. Proctour, who wrote an account of Wyatt's rebellion, in which he mentions Sir Andrew as helping to quell the insurrection, was a fellow of All Souls' College, Oxford. Sir Andrew himself

His choice of the first Head Master.

[1] Vide page 77.

had a brother there at the same time with Proctour, and it is not impossible that the connexion of that College with the School may have influenced his election; however, the Founder's intention, as to the religion to be preserved in his School is distinctly, though cautiously expressed in the original statutes by the words,—" I will .... that the masters should teach the religion now (in 1553[1]) publickly set forth "—i. e. the Protestant; and this (in 1564), a few years after Sir Andrew's death, was confirmed by the supervision and approval[2] of these statutes by Archbishop Parker and Alexander Nowell, Dean of St. Paul's, who were both staunch reformers.

[1] In 1549 a Book of Common Prayer was first used, but from 1553 to 1558 this was suppressed by Queen Mary.
[2] Vide page 57.

SIR THOMAS SMYTHE

Sir Thomas Smythe's parentage and sons.

SIR THOMAS SMYTHE was the third son of Customer Smythe and Alice Judde, and therefore one of the Founder's grandsons. He was a great benefactor to the School and to the poor of Tonbridge. Of his two sons, the one married the youngest daughter of the Earl of Warwick, the other married the widow of the Earl of Sunderland, who, when Lady Dorothy Sydney, was celebrated by Waller under the name of "Sacharissa." She was the mother of Robert Smythe, the grandfather of Lord Chief Baron Sir Sydney Stafford Smythe, who died in 1778.

He became a well known man in London.

Sir Thomas was governour of the Company trading to the East Indies, and treasurer for the colony of Virginia. In 1600 he was Sheriff of London, and four years afterwards he became ambassador at the Court of Russia in the reign of James I.; he was also Secretary of State for twenty years, and the only layman in the Council which the Bishops held for the correction of the Liturgy in the reign of Elizabeth.

While holding these appointments, he had a splendid mansion at Deptford, and afterwards he took the manor of Southborough, near Tonbridge, called "Bounds," at present the seat of Sir Henry Hardinge, Bart., but, later in his life, he resided at Sutton-at-Hone, near Dartford in Kent, where he had an estate.

He had a house at Deptford,
At Southborough,
And at Dartford.

There are one or two extracts from old books of interest about him. Thus Winwood in his Memorials, vol. iii. p. 118, 1609, says, "Our East India merchants have lately built a goodly ship of above 1200 tun, to the launching whereof the King and Prince were invited and had a bountiful banquett. The King presented Sir Thomas Smythe, the governour, with a chaine, in manner of a collar, better than 200*l*., with his picture hanging at it, and put it about his neck with his own hand, naming the great ship 'Trades' Increase,' and the Prince, a pinnace of 250 tun (built to wait upon her), 'Peppercorn.'"

Extracts from old books about him.

Another book, written anonymously and without Sir Thomas's knowledge, gives a detailed account of his Russian transactions in 1604. Its title is "Sir Thomas Smythe's Voyage and Entertainments in Russia; with the Tragical End of Two Emperors and One Empress, within One Month, during his being there."

The manor of Southborough passed from the family of the Smythes about 1754, but Sir Thomas died at his other estate, near Dartford, Sept. 4, 1625, and was buried in the Church of Sutton-at-Hone, where is the following epitaph, which gives the principal features of his life :—

He died near Dartford, and was buried there.

"To the glorie of God and the pious memorie of the Honourable Sir Thomas Smythe, Knt., late Governour of the East Indian, Muscovian, French, and Sommer Islands

The epitaph in memory of him.

Companies; Treasurer of the Virginia Plantation; Prime Undertaker in the yeare 1612 for that noble designe the discoverie of the North-West Passage; Principal Commissioner for the London Expedition against the Pirates, for a Voyage to the River Senega on the Coaste of Africa. One of the Cheefe Commissioners for the Navie Roiall, and sometyme Ambassadour from the Majestie of Greate Britaine to the Emperour and Greate Duke of Russia and Muscovia; who, havinge judiciouslie, conscionably, and with admirable facilitie, managed many difficult and weightie affaires, to the honour and proffit of this nation, rested from his labours the fowrth daie of Sept. 1625; and, his soule returninge to Him that gave it, his bodie is layd up here, in the hope of a blessed resurrection.

"From those large kingdomes where the sunne doth rise;
From that rich newfounde world that westward lyes;
From Volga to the Floud of Amazones;
From under both the Poles and all the Zones;
From all the famous rivers, landes, and seas,
Betwixt this place and our Antipodes;
He gott intelligence what mighte be founde
To give contentment through this massie rounde.
But findinge earthlie thinges did rather tire,
His longinge soule then answerd her desire:
To this obscured village he withdrewe,
From hence his heavenly voyage did persewe;
Here summd up all, and when his gale of breth
Had left becalmed in the porte of dethe
The soules frayl barke, and safe had landed her,
(Where Faith, his factor and his harbinger,

Made place before,) he did noe doubt obtaine
That welth which here on earthe wee seek in vaine."

Sir Thomas Smythe was a great benefactor to the School. By his will, dated April 18, 1619, he bequeathed to the Skinners' Company houses in Old Change and in Lime Street, London, to dispose of their revenues according to his will. By this means, he was able to direct that the Head Master's salary should be increased by ten pounds, and the Usher's by five pounds. He also founded six Exhibitions of ten pounds per annum to last seven years, now increased to fifteen pounds each, by accumulated amounts unapplied in former years through want of applicants, in aid of "the maintenance of six poor scholars at the Universities, who shall be most towardly and capable of learning, and who shall have been brought up and taught in the said School by the space of three years." During their University Education, these Exhibitioners were to study divinity, and afterwards to enter the "sacred ministry." When ordained as clergymen, they were required before and after their sermons to give thanks to God for His mercy toward them in the contribution of their benefactor for their maintenance, for the reason that it should excite others to do good and charitable works.

A third gift of 6*l*. 13*s*. 4*d*. per annum was given by Sir Thomas Smythe to the Skinners' Company towards defraying the expenses of their annual visit to Tonbridge, for which purpose the founder had only left forty shillings. It is probable that Sir Thomas felt that this duty should not go unrewarded, so as in course of time to become a burden. In those days this visit to Tonbridge involved a forty miles' ride on the first Tuesday in May, and the same distance back again on the following evening; and it was not unlikely that to some of the visitors such an exertion would be neither a pleasure nor a holiday, but two hard days' work. For these reasons, probably, he left a sum more than three times the amount of that left by Sir Andrew Judde for the same purpose.

His arrangements for the right distribution of his gifts.

The business-like way in which Sir Thomas went to work is worthy of all praise. Thus, having made his will, he proceeds to add, that as bequests are frequently mistaken, and not carried out according to the real purpose and wish of the donor, therefore on the 1st day of May, after making his will, he would deliver yearly to the Company of Skinners during his lifetime the above-mentioned sums, to be expended as directed. Besides this, he was probably aware that a small school of perhaps thirty or forty boys could not all at once send up six "towardly" and fit scholars to the Universities; therefore, for the first year, one scholar only was to be chosen; for the second, two; and so on, till the full number of six was completed.

The Visitation Sermon preached before him in 1620.

In the first year of his gift, May, 1620, Thomas Gataker, B.D., then vicar of Rotherhithe, a famous preacher and one of the most learned men of his time, delivered the annual Visitation Sermon at the parish church of Tonbridge. It was addressed to Sir Thomas Smythe in his presence; and Gataker, in his discourse, forcibly grasped the peculiarly good point in Sir Thomas's benefaction in the following words[1]:—"The School," said he, "was first erected and endowed by your pious ancestor. And you have worthily built upon his foundation, and added liberally to his

---

[1] Gataker's Sermons were published in 1637.

gift; so that, through your munificence, it is very likely to flourish, and not come behind some of those that be of chief note. Your bounty herein, and in other works of the like nature, is the rather to be regarded for that you do not (as is the manner of the most, unwilling to part with aught till they must needs leave all) defer wholly your well-doing to your death's bed or your dying day, but bend yourself thereunto, while you may yet, surviving your own donation, yourself see things settled in due course, and receive comfort by view of the fruit that may thereby redound both to church and commonwealth."

Again, speaking of Sir Thomas, he added, he "hath given a large and liberal exhibition for the maintenance of seven scholars in one of the Universities to be chosen successively each year from your school." Besides these charities, Sir Thomas bequeathed the surplus of his property to be distributed among certain different parishes—as bread to the poor of Tonbridge and clothes to almsmen.

The amount of revenue from Sir Thomas's property was, about 1789, 140*l.* per annum; in 1820, 152*l.*; since then 340*l.* per annum; and in 1867, 600*l.* The Skinners' Company recently applied to the Court of Chancery for permission to increase the amount of the Exhibitions; they were not, however, successful in this application, but were refused on the ground that the surplus was already willed to these parishes. It is clear that, by this decision, the donor's purpose is defeated; since the value of his gift to the School is depreciated by the fact that no one can hold a Smythe Exhibition together with a Judde one: the consequence is, that as there are four of the latter and six of the former, the Smythe Exhibitions are frequently vacant

[margin: The revenues from his property; the Skinners' Company desired to utilize it more effectually, but were unable to do so.]

through want of applicants, as the School does not send up an average of ten boys a year to the Universities. The advantage to the parishes is simply that it relieves them in some degree from the duty of taking care of themselves, and pays a portion of their poor-rates.

HENRY FISHER

SIR ANDREW JUDDE having bought property to found the School, and having completed the act of foundation, intended during his lifetime to have handed it over formally to the Skinners' Company. But, in purchasing the property, Sir Andrew "of trust" joined with himself Henry Fisher, his servant. Sir Andrew dying before the completion of the conveyance of this property, Henry Fisher completed it according to the founder's well-known intentions. In addition to this, he himself made a gift to the Company of several houses, out of the rents of which they were annually to pay a certain sum (now twenty pounds) for a scholarship at Brazenose College, Oxford, the residue remaining with the Company. Henry Fisher conveys the Founder's property to the Company, and makes a donation to them,

This gift, like that of Sir Thomas Smythe, was also made during the donor's lifetime; and the purpose of it was, that "whereas Henry Fisher had placed one John Wheland, some time a scholar of the School at Tunbridge, at Brazen-

From which they had to provide a scholarship.

nose College, Oxford, the Company of Skinners should pay for ever to Wheland and his successors (appointed by Fisher while alive, and after his death by the Company) the yearly sum of 2*l*. 13*s*. 4*d*.; to his tutor, 13*s*. 4*d*.; and to the College itself, 1*l*. 13*s*. 4*d*.; to the end they might be good to such scholar as should be there from time to time found and placed, and to the end they might be aiding and assisting to the said Masters, Wardens, and commonalty in choosing and providing a meet and convenient schoolmaster and usher to the said School of Tunbridge when need should be required, and they thereunto require."

SIR THOMAS WHITE

SIR THOMAS WHITE, Founder of St. John's College, Oxford, out of friendship and esteem for Andrew Judde, gave to Tonbridge School a Fellowship at his College. The inhabitants of Tonbridge used to elect the candidate, and the competitors canvassed the townspeople for their votes[1]. The Fellowship was a probationary one for three years, after which time the holder became a "verus et perpetuus socius." It was of different value in different years, averaging about 75*l.*, and the Fellowship to which it used to lead is on the same footing as the other Fellowships of St. John's College, and rises in value gradually, according to the standing of the holder, from about 100*l.* a year to three or four times that amount. In 1859 it was thrown open to competition, on account of no Tonbridge boy qualifying, and was gained

Sir Thomas White's Fellowship.

[1] The words in the College statutes are "proctores vel seniores," which only apply to corporate towns, and were meant to apply to Coventry, Bristol, and Reading. Tonbridge is not a corporate town; the words probably were intended to refer to the principal executive authority in the place.

and is now held by C. E. C. B. Appleton, B.C.L. The University Commission, when drawing up their Report on St. John's College in 1858, recommended that the Fellowships should be thrown open, and some of them changed into Scholarships. The reasons given for the proposed change were—(1) that tuition would be more efficient with open Fellowships; (2) that the College would get less good candidates for its open Fellowships if the majority of them were close; and (3) that it is undesirable that a College should be permanently governed by a Society of which the majority must be chosen from so confined a circle as it necessarily must be if the Fellowships remain close. The ultimate result of this was, that an Ordinance, framed by a Committee of Privy Council especially appointed for the purpose, was imposed on the College. This changed the fifty Fellowships then existing into eighteen Fellowships and thirty-three Scholarships. In this way the Tonbridge Fellowship has now become a Scholarship of the value of 100*l.* a year, which will not be open to competition whilst Mr. Appleton retains his Fellowship.

<small>The change it has undergone.</small>

An extract from Sir Thomas White's Statutes of St. John's College, Oxford, gives the particulars of the gift :—

<small>Extract from St. John's College Statutes.</small>

"Also, every of these particular schools, namely of Coventry, Bristol, and Redding, shall have two scholars, which shall be partakers of the same commodities and privileges which the rest have. Let there be one also chosen out of Tunbridge School in the county of Kent. And now to the end there may be some certainty appointed concerning the nominating and electing these seven scholars, which we will have equal to the rest in all the commodities and privileges of the college, as often as any place of these seven shall happen to be void, we will, that within forty days after such avoydance, the president and fellows shall certify and advertize by letters, signed with their own hands, the magistrates of those places out of the which such scholars are to be named and chosen concerning the same; for there are out of these several cities or towns, Coventry, Bristol, Redding, and Tunbridge, two to be elected (except out of Tunbridge, out of which, in respect of great love we did bear Andrew Judd, Knighte, builder of the grammar school there, we do ordain and will, that one scholar shall be nominated and elected as often as the place assigned for this school shall happen to be void), and they shall have a care to send such out of their schools to the college, whom either they shall themselves know, or in the judgment of others shall be fit to learn logic."

ROBERT HOLMEDON

Robert Holmedon's Exhibition.

AN Exhibition of 4*l.*, now increased to about 35*l.* a year, tenable for four years, was left by Robert Holmedon to a scholar of Sevenoaks School, and in default of one from that place, to a scholar from Tonbridge School, in the appointment of the Leathersellers' Company.

THOMAS LAMPARD

Thomas Lampard's Exhibition.

THOMAS LAMPARD was a yeoman of Tonbridge. He gave an Exhibition of the value of four marcs (2*l.* 13*s.* 4*d.*) to a poor scholar going to either university, in the nomination of the Head Master, and on the appointment of the vicar and churchwardens of the town. This small sum was annually charged upon a house and lands at Lamberhurst, in Kent, and was paid by the proprietor of the premises to the scholar himself. It is payable now by Frederic Smith, Esquire, out of the Brewery Estate, Lamberhurst, Kent.

LADY MARY BOSWELL

LADY MARY BOSWELL, by a deed of endowment dated 1675, bequeathed a farm, called Holywell, near Burnham in Essex, to furnish two Exhibitions of 12*l.* a year, now increased to about 50*l.* each, tenable for four years, at Jesus College, Cambridge. These were to be given to boys at Tonbridge, in default of any from Sevenoaks School. Tonbridge, however, has rarely, if ever, held these Exhibitions.

[margin: Lady Boswell's bequest.]

MINOR EXHIBITIONS

THERE were one or two small bequests originally left to the School, but which from their unimportance, and the length of time which has passed since they were given, have altogether disappeared. For instance, a Mr. Worrall left two Exhibitions of 6*l.* to the School, in the election of the master and seniors of St. John's College, Cambridge. A Mr. Strong left, in the last century, a sum of money "for the apprenticing to some marine business of a scholar educated at the great School in Tonbridge." This money has never been known to have been made use of. It is placed to the credit of the School income on the books of the Governours, and Dr. Welldon wishes to apply it to the formation of an Exhibition for a boy intended for the navy, engineering, ship-building, or something of that kind. Besides these, there are two Exhibitions of 50*l.* annually, given by the Head and Second Masters, for boys under fourteen years of age, each tenable for two years, after which time they are thrown open to all the School.

[margin: Smaller donations.]

[margin: And Exhibitions.]

THE SKINNERS' COMPANY

The Skinners' Company.

THE Company of Skinners, as has been already stated, were entrusted with the administration of the funds of the School from the time of its foundation.

In the same year that Sir Andrew Judde was Lord Mayor (1551) he was also Master of the Company, then in its greatest prosperity. The full title under which it was incorporated in 1327 was "The Master and Wardens of the Guild or Fraternity of the Body of Christ of the Skinners of London." (See Herbert, "History of the Twelve City Companies.") It has numbered among its members six kings, five queens, one prince, nine dukes, two earls, one

Their title.

Eminent members.

baron, and seventeen lord mayors. On the annual "Gaudy Day" of the Company the following ceremony was performed by the members, according to Stowe in his "Survey of London," vol. ii. bk. v. :— *Their annual festival.*

"Once in every year, on Corpus Christi day, they had a procession, which passed through the principal streets of the city, wherein were borne more than 100 torches of wax, costly garnished, burning light, and above 200 Clerks and Priests, in surplisses and copes, singing; after the which were the Sheriffs' Servants—the Clerks of the Compters—Chaplains of the Sheriffs—the Mayor's Serjeants—the Council of the City—the Mayor and Aldermen in scarlet—and then the Skinners in their best liveries. This procession has long fallen into disuse, but the Holiday of Corpus Christi is still observed as a festival by the Company, when their officers are appointed, and their annual charities bestowed."

There is such an excellent reason given in Carlisle's "Endowed Grammar Schools" (vol. ii. p. 83) for entrusting the management of a School to a Merchant Company, that justice to the foresight of Sir Andrew Judde demands its insertion here. The subject is Dean Colet's leaving St. Paul's School, of which he was the Founder, to the care of the Mercers' Company. *Dean Colet approved of placing Schools under the care of a City Company,*

"After he (Dean Colet) had finished all, he left the perpetual care of the estate and the government of it, not to the Clergy, not to the Bishop, not to the Chapter, nor to any great minister at Court, but among the married laymen of the Court of Mercers—men of probity and reputation; and when he was asked the reason of so committing the trust, he answered to the effect that there was

Because they were less liable to misappropriate the trust than any single person.

no absolute certainty in human affairs, but, for his part, he found less corruption in such a body of citizens than in any other order or degree of mankind."

The following is a list of the Governours of the School for the year 1869-70:—

Master.
William Halse Gatty Jones.

Wardens.

Archibald Frederick Paull.	Robert Henry Parkinson.
Henry Simmonds.	James F. Wadmore.
Benjamin Rowsell.	Benjamin Richard Aston.
Charles Barry.	Joseph Causton, Alderman.
William Knox Child.	George Legg.
Skinner Zachary Langton.	George Trist.
Jonah Smith Wells.	Frederick Howell.
Henry Buckle.	Samuel Wix.
James L. Reynolds.	Edwin Lawrence Poland.
John Locke, Q.C., M.P.	Frederic Turner.
Henry William Lord.	Skinner Row.
John Fulling Turner.	Emanuel Silva.
John Alldin Moore.	William Scott.

CHARTER TO SIR ANDREW JUDDE

FOR THE FOUNDATION OF A GRAMMAR SCHOOL AT TONBRIDGE, IN THE COUNTY OF KENT, 7TH EDWARD VI., 1553.

THE King To all to whom &c. greeting know ye that we, at the humble petition of Sir Andrew Judd, Knight, and Alderman of our City of London, for the erecting and establishing a Grammar School in the Town of Tonbridge in the County of Kent for the institution and instruction of boys and youth in the said Town and the County there adjacent, of our special grace and of our certain knowledge and mere motion do will, grant and ordain that from henceforth there may and shall be one Grammar School in the said Town of Tonbridge which shall be called the Free Grammar School of the aforesaid Sir Andrew Judd, Knight, in the said Town of Tonbridge, for the education institution and instruction of Boys and Youth in Grammar, to continue for ever. And the same School of one Master or Pedagogue and the under Master or Usher to

Of a Grant to Sir Andrew Judde concerning a Free School.

continue for ever we do erect create and found by these presents. And that the intent aforesaid may the better take effect, and that the lands, tenements, rent, revenues, and other things to be granted assigned and appointed towards the support of the School aforesaid may the better be governed for the continuance of the same School, we will and ordain that from henceforth the aforesaid Sir Andrew Judd during his natural life shall be and be called Governor of the Possessions, Revenues and Goods of the said School; and after the death of the aforesaid Sir Andrew Judd we will and ordain that the Master, Warden and Commonalty of the Mistery of the Skinners of London, for the time being shall be and be called Governors of the Possessions, Revenues and Goods of the said School commonly called and to be called The Free Grammar School of the said Sir Andrew Judd. And therefore know ye that we have assigned, elected, nominated and constituted, and by these presents do assign, elect, nominate and constitute the aforesaid Sir Andrew Judd to be the first and present Governor of the Possessions, Revenues and Goods of the said Free Grammar School, well and faithfully to exercise and occupy the same office during his natural life, and after the death of the said Sir Andrew Judd the aforesaid Master, Wardens and Commonalty of the Mistery of Skinners of London, aforesaid, and their successors, for the time being, well and faithfully to exercise and occupy the same office from the death of the aforesaid Sir Andrew Judd for ever. And that the same Sir Andrew Judd during his natural life may and shall be Governor in deed, fact and name, during his life may and shall be a body corporate and politic of himself, by the name of Governor of the Possessions, Revenues and Goods of

The Founder to be Governour of the School, and after his death the Skinners' Company to take his place.

the Free Grammar School of the aforesaid Sir Andrew Judd, Knight, incorporated and erected; and the same Sir Andrew Judd Governor of the Possessions, Revenues and Goods of the said Free Grammar School during his life by these presents we do incorporate and a body corporate and politic by the same name really and fully to do create, erect, ordain, make and constitute by these presents. And we will that after the death of the aforesaid Sir Andrew Judd the same Master, Wardens and Commonalty of the Mistery of the Skinners of London aforesaid and their Successors, may and shall be Governors of the said School in deed, fact and name, and from thenceforth may and shall be one body corporate and politic of themselves for ever, by the name of Governors of the Possessions, Revenues and Goods of the Free Grammar School of the aforesaid Sir Andrew Judd, Knight, incorporated and erected; and the same Master, Wardens and Commonalty and their Successors Governors of the Possessions, Revenues and Goods of the said Free Grammar School after the death of the aforesaid Sir Andrew Judd for ever by these presents we do incorporate and a body corporate and politic of the same name to endure for ever really and fully, we do create, erect, ordain, make and constitute by these presents. And further we will and by these presents ordain and grant that the same Sir Andrew Judd, Governor during his life of the Possessions, Revenues and Goods of the said Free Grammar School, by the same name may and shall be a person able and capable in the law during his life to have and receive for the term of his life, as well of us, our heirs and successors, as of any other person or persons whomsoever, lands, tenements and hereditaments whatsoever towards the support

Sir Andrew's title to be "Governour of the Possessions, Revenues, and Goods of the School," and the Skinners' Company to take the same name.

of the School aforesaid, the remainder thereof to the aforesaid Master, Wardens and Commonalty of the Mistery of Skinners and their successors, for the support aforesaid. And also we will and by these presents ordain and grant that after the death of the aforesaid Sir Andrew Judd, Knight, the aforesaid Master, Wardens and Commonalty of the Mistery of Skinners of London aforesaid, for the time being shall be Governors of the Possessions, Revenues and Goods of the said Free Grammar School, and shall have perpetual succession, and by the same name may and shall be personable and capable in law to have and receive lands, tenements, meadows, feedings, pastures, rents, reversions and revenues and hereditaments whatsoever, as well of us our heirs or successors, as of the said Sir Andrew Judd his heirs, executors or assigns, or of any other person or persons whomsoever in like manner towards the support of the School aforesaid. And further we will and for us, our heirs and successors, grant by these presents to the aforesaid Governors and their successors that from henceforth they shall have a common seal to serve for their business touching or concerning only the premises and other things in these Letters Patent expressed and specified, or any parcel thereof, and that the same Governors by the name of Governors of the Possessions, Revenues and Goods of the Free Grammar School of the aforesaid Sir Andrew Judd, Knight, in Tunbridge, aforesaid, shall be able to plead and be impleaded, defend and be defended, answer and be answered, in whatsoever courts and places and before whatsoever judges in whatsoever causes, actions, business, suits, plaints, pleas and demand of whatsoever nature or condition they may be, touching or concerning the premises or any parcel thereof,

The Governours are to be a corporate body,

And to have a common seal.

or for any offences, trespasses, things, causes or matters by any person or persons done or perpetrated, or to be done or perpetrated in or upon the premises, or any parcel thereof, or any thing in these presents specified. And moreover of our further grace and of our certain knowledge and mere motion we have given and granted, and by these presents do give and grant, to the aforesaid Sir Andrew Judd, the the present Governor during his natural life, full power and authority to nominate and appoint the Master and Under Master of the School aforesaid, so often as the same School shall be void of a Master, and that the same Sir Andrew Judd during his life from time to time shall make and shall and may be able to make fit and wholesome Statutes and Ordinances in writing concerning and touching the order, government and direction of the Master and Under Master and Scholars of the School aforesaid, for the time being, and the stipend and salary of the same Master and Under Master, and other things touching and concerning the same School, and the order, governance, preservation and disposition of the rents and revenues to be appointed for the support of the same School, which same Statutes and Ordinances so to be made we will grant, and by these presents command, to be inviolably observed from time to time for ever. And moreover we have given and granted, and by these presents do give and grant, to the aforesaid Master, Wardens and Commonalty of the Mistery of Skinners of London, and their successors and the major part for the time being, that they, after the death of the aforesaid Sir Andrew Judd, Knight, shall have full power and authority to nominate and appoint the Master and Under Master of the School aforesaid, so often as the

[margin: Their power as regards the appointment of the Masters and their salaries;]

[margin: The drawing up of Statutes,]

said School shall be void of a Master and Under Master; and that the same Governors, with the advice of the Warden and Fellows of the College of All Saints, in the University of Oxford, for the time being, from time to time shall and may be able to make, if need shall be, fit and wholesome Statutes and Ordinances in writing, concerning and touching the order, government and direction of the Master and Under Master and Scholars of the School aforesaid, for the time being, and other things touching and concerning the same School, and the order, government, preservation and disposition of the rents and revenues to be appointed for the support of the same School; which same Statutes and Ordinances so to be made we will grant, and by these presents command, inviolably to be observed from time to time for ever. And, moreover, of our further grace we have given and granted, and by these presents do give and grant, for us, our heirs and successors, to the aforesaid Master, Wardens and Commonalty of the Mistery of Skinners of London aforesaid, and their successors, special licence and free and lawful faculty, power and authority, to have, receive and purchase to them and their successors for ever, towards the support and maintenance of the School aforesaid, as well of us, our heirs or successors, as of the aforesaid Sir Andrew Judd, Knight, or of any other person and persons whomsoever manors, messuages, lands, tenements, rectories, tithes and other hereditaments whatever within our kingdom of England, or elsewhere within our Dominions, provided they shall not exceed the yearly value of forty pounds; any Statute concerning lands and tenements not to be put into Mortmain, or any other Statute, Act, Ordinance, or Provision, or any other thing, cause, or matter whatsoever to the con-

And the general management of the School property.

trary thereof, had made, enacted, ordained, or provided in any wise notwithstanding. And we will and by these presents ordain that all the issues, rents and revenues of all the lands, tenements and possessions hereafter to be given and assigned towards the support of the School aforesaid from time to time, shall be converted to the support of the Master and Under Master of the School aforesaid for the time being, and to the reparation of the said lands and tenements, and not otherwise nor to any other uses or intents. And we will and by these presents grant to the aforesaid Governors that they may and shall have these our Letters Patent under our Great Seal of England in due manner made and sealed without fine or fee great or small to us in our Hanaper, or elsewhere to our use, for the same in any wise to be rendered, paid or done although express mention &c. In witness whereof &c. Witness the King at Westminster the sixteenth day of May in the seventh year of his reign.

Application of the School revenues.

By Writ of Privy Seal.

THE FOUNDATION OF THE SCHOOL AND ITS REVENUES

The object of the Charter is explained.

SIR ANDREW JUDDE procured a grant by Letters Patent of the 7th of King Edward VI., 1553, for the purpose of erecting and establishing a Grammar School for the instruction of boys in the town of Tonbridge and the county there adjacent[1]. The School was to be called "The Free Grammar School of Sir Andrew Judde, for the education, institution, and instruction of boys and youths in grammar, to continue for ever, under one Master and Usher." Sir Andrew was appointed Governour of the School and of its revenues and possessions during his lifetime, with power to appoint and remove the Master and Usher, and to fix their salaries. After his death the Master, Wardens, and Commonalty of the Skinners' Company were to be Governours, under the name of "Governours of the possessions, revenues, and goods of the Free

The Skinners' Company to be Governours of the School

---

[1] Baker's Chronicles, ed. 1783, p. 311. Hasted's History of Kent, vol. ii. p. 336.

Grammar School of Sir Andrew Judde," with the same power vested in them, after the Founder's death, as he had himself had during his lifetime. <small>after the death of the Founder, and the School property is placed under their control.</small>

Sir Andrew Judde empowered the Governours, with the advice of the Warden and Fellows of "All Saints'[1]" College, Oxford, to administer the affairs of the School, and to apply the revenues solely to the purpose of maintaining the Master and Usher, and of keeping up the School revenues.

The property thus given to the Skinners' Company, to hold in trust for the School, comprised some houses in Gracechurch Street, valued at 30*l.* per annum, and about three acres of what was then pasture-land in the Parish of St. Pancras. This was called the "Sandhills," and was bought by the Founder for 346*l.* 6*s.* 8*d.* It is now covered with streets deriving their names from villages around Tonbridge, as Bidborough, Hadlow, Speldhurst, &c. <small>The School property in London.</small>

But Sir Andrew thought fit to execute a will as well as his previous Charter. In this will, dated Sept. 2, 1558, Sir Andrew repeated his gift to the School, and added a further gift on different conditions. This consisted of a house in Old Swan Alley, one in St. Helen's, several in St. Mary Axe, and an annual rent-charge of ten pounds out of a messuage in Gracechurch Street. The conditions were that this property should help together with the School property to defray the expenses of the School; and after that, the surplus of this latter property held by the Skinners' Company under the will was to go to the Company's general fund. However, as the revenues of the School were for a long time insufficient to meet its expenses, and as the Company had gratuitously paid the deficiency from their own <small>Sir Andrew Judde's will.</small>

---

[1] All Souls', vide p. 74.

private funds, there was for a long time no question about a surplus. But when, in 1819, the property began to be let out on very much more favourable leases, and the revenues amounted to about 4000*l*. per annum, the Skinners' Company claimed the surplus income of the property left by the will.

The increase of the property raised a question as to the disposition of the surplus,

This claim was resisted by the School, and Dr. Thomas Knox, the Head Master then, was of opinion that the surplus revenues should be given to the Head Master and Usher. This, however, was not allowed, and the matter was ultimately decided in Chancery. The result was the new Scheme[1] for the establishment of the School, put in force in 1825, at which time the financial difficulty was set at rest. The Company had no claim on the money dedicated by the letters patent, but only on the surplus of the money added by the will, of which no mention was made in the letters patent; so the surplus of this, after defraying certain expenses of the School, was decided to belong to the Skinners' Company. The revenues, arising from the Founder's property, at the time when it passed into the hands of the Governours of the School, is thus valued by Stowe[2]: "Sir Andrew Judde left to the Skinners' Company lands the value of threescore pounds, three shillings, and eight pence yearly for maintenance; and four shillings a week for six poor men, and twenty shillings a year for coals for the School." In Queen Elizabeth's reign an account was drawn up of the expenditure of several Companies. In the account returned of the expenditure of the Skinners' Company, three items are charged:—

Which produced the Scheme of 1825.

The original income of the School.

"To the Master and Usher of the Schole of Tonbridge,

[1] Vide p. 161.
[2] Strype's Stowe's Survey of London, vol. i. bk. i. p. 263; vol. ii. bk. v. p. 274.

the reparations of the same, and the charges at the examination of the Schollers of the said Schole yearlie, 11*l*. 2*s*. 6*d*. Six Schollers maintained at Oxford and Cambridge cost us yearlie 30*l*. In Exhibitions to Schollers, 13*l*. 6*s*. 8*d*. To the maintenance of the Schole, 33*l*. 6*s*. 8*d*."

In 1560, two years after Sir Andrew's death, Henry Fisher, joint trustee with the Founder, in due course proceeded to convey the property, together with some additional property of his own, to the Company as Governours of the School. Thus Henry Fisher fulfilled the Founder's wishes, and the property was formally passed to the Skinners' Company in 1561. Henry Fisher, however, left a son named Andrew, who, after his father's death, forged a document pretending to have been made by his father in 1560, the purport of which was that, in 1560, previously to the real conveyance to the Skinners' Company, Henry Fisher, joining with himself the Bishop of Ely, had limited the uses of the Founder's property to himself for sixty years, and after that, or on Henry Fisher's death, it was to pass as a legacy to Andrew Fisher. This atrocious attempt to dispossess the School of its property was happily frustrated; the matter was brought before Parliament in 1572, by a brother of Andrew, named Henry, and the following entry is to be found in the Journals of the House of Commons:—

Henry Fisher passed the property to the Company,

But his son disputed the transfer,

But his object was defeated.

"Lunae, 13mo Junii, 1572. It is this day ordered upon the question, that touching the Bill passed in this House for the School of Tunbridge and Andrew Fisher, these words following should be set down: viz. Memorandum, that the said Bill, in which one deed was made in the name of Henry Fisher, is supposed to be forged, was committed to the Right Hon. Sir Walter Mildmay, Chancellor, &c.,

Report of the House of Commons on the subject,

and others, who have certified to the House that they have found great untruth and impudency in the said Andrew Fisher, and that for very vehement presumptions they think very evil of the deed: nevertheless, upon Fisher's submission, they have consented to draw out of the Bill all words that touched him in infamy, and so the Bill penned and passed this House with assent on both sides, as well to help Tunbridge School, and others that had bought land of the said Andrew Fisher's father *bonâ fide*.

Which severely condemns Andrew Fisher.

"And the said Committees have further reported that the said matter coming also into question in the Higher House, before Committees there, at the suit of Henry, brother of the said Andrew, the Committees of the Higher House have, for great causes, agreed in opinion with the Committees of this House concerning the deed."

Andrew Fisher, not content with this, set up further claims to the property, on the ground that the name of the Company was not properly styled in his father's conveyance. Hence a second Act of Parliament was passed in 1589, enacting that the Company should be called, as regarded the School, "Governours of the possessions, revenues, and goods of the Free Grammar Schoole of Sir Andrew Judde, Knight, in the town of Tunbridge in the county of Kent." Fuller, in his "Worthies of England," says that "this fair School hath been twice founded in effect, seeing the defence and maintenance thereof hath cost the Company of Skinners, in suits of law and otherwise, 4000*l.*, so careful have they been, though to their own great charge, to see the will of the dead performed[1]."

The expense the Governours were put to in defending the School.

The present annual income of the School is about 3600*l.*,

[1] Strype's Stowe's Survey of London, vol. ii. bk. v. p. 61.

and when the rents of the property in London fall in again, which they will do in 1890 and 1906, the total amount available for annual expenditure has been estimated by the Skinners' Company at 20,000*l.*, and by Mr. Gladstone at 80,000*l.*: the truth lies most likely between the two; but it is certain that the increase will be very considerable.

ORIGINAL STATUTES OF THE SCHOOL OF TONBRIDGE

Be it known to all Christian People, by this present Writings indented, That whereas I, Sir Andrew Judd, Knight and Alderman of London, have erected a Free[1] Grammar School in the town of Tunbridge, in the county of Kent, for the bringing up the youth in virtue and learning; for the better accomplishment of the same, I have appointed certain Orders to be observed, as hereafter doth follow.

The Master to be chosen

Imprimis, I require that the Master of the said School be whole of body, well reputed, Master of Arts in degree, if it may be, chosen by my trusty and well-beloved Friends the

---

[1] "'A Free School' formerly meant one where a genteel and liberal education is given, and not free of cost merely, and is opposed to inferior schools where mechanical or low qualifications are taught."—Knox's Liberal Education. "Free from the jurisdiction of a superior corporation; almost all existing were obnoxius—attached and subservient to chapters or colleges, more or less dependent on ecclesiastical power."—B. H. Kennedy, D.D., Shrewsbury Journal, September 15, 1860.

Company of the Skinners of London, to whose direction I commit the governance of this my said School and Orders. Always foreseen that the Schoolmaster and Usher teach the Grammar approved by the Queen's Majesty that now is, and that the Schoolmaster first allowed by the Ordinary, and by examination be found meet both for his learning and his dexterity in teaching, as also for his honest conversation, and for right understanding of God's true religion now set forth by public authority, whereunto he shall stir and move his scholars, and also shall prescribe to them such sentences of Holy Scripture as shall be most expedient to induce them to godliness. *By the Skinners' Company. And to give religious instruction to the scholars.*

Item, I will that the Master always appoint and elect the Usher as often as the place shall be void, whom so appointed and presented to the said Company of Skinners, I desire them to admit him, not knowing sufficient cause to refuse him. *The Master to elect the Usher.*

Item, I will that the Master receive quarterly for his wages *Five Pounds*[1] and the Usher *Forty Shillings*, to be delivered by the hands of the said Skinners or their Deputy; and that they have their dwelling rent free and all other charges, as in repairing of the said School, in all manner of reparations borne and allowed necessarily, and according to the view from time to time taken yearly by the said Wardens. *The Master's and Usher's salary.*

Item, I will that the Master and Usher have their houses and wages during their lives, not sufficiently convicted to have neglected their office. And if it happen either of them

---

[1] The salary of the Head Master of St. Paul's School about the same time was "a mark a weke and a levery gowne of iiii nobles delivered in cloth."—Knight's Life of Colet, ed. 1724, p. 358.

The Master to be removed in certain cases. to be so convicted at any time, yet I will not that he be straightly removed, but gently warned and admonished, and so for the second time; and that then, if after the second admonition he do not amend, and diligently follow his office and charge in the School, I require that he so offending be utterly expulsed and removed, and another to be received in his room; and to be done with all diligence by the said Company of Skinners.

Both to conduct themselves decorously. Item, I will that the Master and Usher shall neither of them be a common gamester or haunter of Taverns, nor by any extraordinary or unnecessary expences in apparel or otherwise become an infamy to the School, and an evil example to the young, to whom in all points they ought to show themselves an example of an honest, continent, and godly behaviour.

The boarding-houses. Item, I, desiring the benefit of the inhabitants of the said Town of Tunbridge, in boarding of Scholars and otherwise, I do will that the Master of the said Grammar School shall not take to board, dyet or lodge in his house or rooms above the number of twelve scholars, and the Usher not to take above the number of eight scholars, unless it shall seem convenient to the Company of Skinners that they upon occasion and consideration may have a greater number at board and lodging with them.

In case of the Master's indisposition, Item, if it happen the Master or Usher to be visited with a common disease, as the ague or any curable sickness, I require that he so visited be tollerated for the time, and his wages fully allowed, so that his office be discharged by his sufficient Deputy. But if (which God forbid) they or any of them fall into any infective and incurable disease, especially through their own evil behaviour, then I will that he so infected be removed and put away, and another to be chosen in his room.

Item, If it happen the Master or Usher, after long time spent in the School, to wax impotent, and unable through age or other infirmities to endure the travell and labour necessary in the School, I require that he be favourably borne withal, so that his office be satisfied by his sufficient Deputy, although he himself be not present. *And in case of superannuation.*

Item, I will that the Master and Usher be at liberty to remain single, or to marry, or to take priesthood, so that he trouble not himself with any care or worldly business that might hinder his office in the School.

Item, I will that if any controversy happen to arise and grow between the Master and the Usher at any time, that they then refer the whole matter to the Master and the Wardens of the Company of Skinners in London, and to their Successors, and they to stand to their order and determination in the same, upon pain of deprivation from their office. *Referee to be appointed in cases of dispute between the Master and Usher;*

Item, I will that neither the Master nor the Usher absent themselves above twenty days in the year from their School, nor so much, but upon good and urgent cause; and in that vacant time *the one* to supply the office upon some good convenient allowance as they can agree. *Neither to absent themselves beyond a fixed period.*

Item, If it happen to be such contagious sickness as the plague or such like, that the School cannot continue, yet nevertheless I will that both the Master and the Usher have their wages fully paid, being always in readiness to teach as soon as GOD shall make such contagious sickness to cease.

Item, If it happen the Master or Usher to dye at any time in their office, I will that their executors or assigns shall *In case the death of the Master.*

receive so much money as for his or their service was due at the hour of his or their death; and in such case the room to be supplied with as much convenient speed as may be, and for the vacant time the survivor to satisfy for the whole charge, and to receive so much as is due for the time.

Admission to the School by examination.

Item, I will that none be taught in this School but first the Master be spoken withall by his or their friends and be allowed by the Master's admission, requiring that the Master do give his or their friends to understand such points of the Statutes as hereafter followeth, and he and they being willing to satisfy the same, the Master shall admit his or their scholars, provided that the scholar shall be able before his admission into the School to write competently, and to read perfectly both English and Latin, and that if the Schoolmaster upon proof and tryal of his capacity and not found meet to learn (*sic*), to signify the same to his friends to remove him; and none to tarry above five years in learning of his grammar, without great cause alledged and allowed by the said Master and Wardens of the Company of Skinners for the time being.

Boarding houses to be licensed by the Head Master.

Item, I will that if the Scholar be no dweller in the towne, that then his friends at unwares shall not place him in any such house to be boarded as the Master shall be able sufficiently to prove by some former act of goodman and wife, that it hath been, and is likely to be hereafter, an occasion of scholars to follow idleness and gaming and other vain pastimes not becoming students; therefore to avoid all such inconveniency, the party that taketh the scholar or scholars to board, shall faithfully promise to the Master before his or their admission, to keep them continually from all unthrifty pastimes and gamings in his house; and further, to let the Master have information in case he know that they be lewdly occupied or to go out of his house, not in any point boulthering up the evil, but seeking as he ought, to have them well occupied.

Item, I will that every scholar at his first admission into the School shall pay sixpence to the common boxe[1], with which money the Master at his discretion shall provide necessary books, to remain in the School for the common use of the scholars. *Admission fee for books.*

Item, I will that as often as any scholar doth absent himself from the School, having no occasion of sickness, or shall be wanting above one day without leave of his Master, he shall at his return pay to the common box so many pence as the days come to. *Fines for absence.*

Item, I will that the Master keep a register and in the same write the name and surname of every scholar at his entering; and that the same Master of the said Free School shall make a true and just account to the said Master and Wardens of Skinners, or two of them, at every year, yearly, of such scholars as have been received into the said School and the names of such as have departed thence, so that a true account may be kept thereof, and the said Governors fully answered of all such money so received. *A register of names to be kept by the Governours and the Master.*

Item, Acknowledging God to be the only Author of all knowledge and virtue, I will that the Master and Usher of this my said School with their scholars, at seven of the clock, do first, devoutly kneeling upon their knees, pray to Almighty God, according to the form by the master prescribed. *The hours of the School work regulated.*

[1] Vide page 64.

In the morning.	Item, I will that after the prayer they both remain in the School, diligently teaching, reading, and interpreting unto eleven of the clock in the forenoon, and not to depart without urgent cause, but in any wise one of them to be present always.
In the afternoon.	Item, I will that by one of the clock after dinner they both resort eftsoons to the School, there to remain till five or six of the clock at night, according to the time of the year, at the discretion of the Master, and then, devoutly kneeling on their knees, to pray in form prescribed.
Latin to be colloquially used;	Item, I will that the Master and Usher do usually speak in the Latin Tongue to their scholars that do understand the same.
And regular periodical examinations by the Head Master to take place.	Item, I will that the Master, twice in a month, examine those that be under the Usher's hands, to understand how they profit and go forward in their learning. Item, I will that the Usher practice and use such order and form in teaching as the Master shall think good.
Remedies may be granted.	Item, I will that the Master, or, in his absence, the Usher, shall not give remedy or leave to play[1], above once in fourteen days, unless the said Governors, or some honourable or worshipful person present in the School shall require it, so it be but once in the week, upon pain of three shillings and four pence for every such default, to be paid by the offender, and to be put into the common box of the School to the use as afore is said.
Religious instruction to be regarded.	Item, I will that all the scholars upon the Sabbath and Holidays resort in due time to Divine Service in the Parish Church of Tunbridge, the Master and Usher, or one of them at the least, being present to oversee them; and I will that

---

[1] Vide page 65.

the Master and Usher do duly every Monday in the morning call to reckoning all such of his scholars as either absent themselves from the Church, or shall come tardie to it, or otherwise use not themselves reverently there in praying; every one of them having a Prayer Book in Latin or English according to the Master's appointment.

Item, Considering that virtue and knowledge by prayse and rewards is in all estates maintained and increased, and especially in youth, I will that every year once, to wit the first or second day after May Day, there be kept in this School disputations upon questions provided by the Master, from one of the clock at afternoon till the evensong time, at which disputations I will the Master desire the Vicar of the towne with one or two other of knowledge, or more, dwelling nigh, to be present in the School, if it please them, to hear the same; the disputations ended, to determine which three of the whole number have done best by the judgment of the Master and learned hearers. And I will that the first allowed have a pen of silver, whole of guilt, the price two shillings and sixpence, the second, a pen of silver parcell guilt, of the value of two shillings, the third, a pen of silver of twenty pence, for their rewards. And then I will that the whole company go in order decently by two and two unto the Parish Church, the three victors to come last, next to the Master and Usher, each of them having a garland upon their heads, provided for the purpose, and in the Church then and there to kneel or stand in some convenient place to be approved by the direction of the Wardens and Master of the School, and to say or sing some convenient psalms or hymns with a collect for the preservation of the Queen's Majesty, and to have some

Annual Disputations to take place.

The prizes to be awarded,

And a service in the Parish Church to finish the ceremony.

honourable remembrance of their Founder, so to be appointed and devised by the Master.

The Master on his departure to leave the School property in statu quo.

Item, It shall not be lawful for the Master or Usher or any of their friends at going away from their office to spoyl beforehand or take away from thence, any such things as are set up and fastened in their house, or houses, and planted in their orchards or gardens, but freely to leave the same with as good will as for their time they have enjoyed the use thereof.

And an inventory of the property to be kept by the Governours.

Item, I will that the Company of Skinners have an inventory in their hands of all things that appertain unto the School, be they books or implements in the Master's or Usher's house, so that at the parting they may be stayed to the School's behalf.

There are to be two certified copies of the Ordinances,

Item, I will that there shall be written word for word two copies of these Ordinances, the one ever to remain in the hands of the Skinners, and the other in the custody of the Master of my said School, or such time as the Master's place is vacant, to remain in the Usher's hands, so that they both may thereby learn what appertaineth to their office; and also, at their admission, they shall promise before honest witnesses to keep and see executed all such points as concern them and their scholars to the uttermost of their power, during all the time that they remain in the office.

Which are to be carefully observed by all parties under certain penalties.

Item, That both the Master and Usher shall endeavour themselves to the continual profitting of all the said scholars of the said Grammar School and of their parts faithfully to observe and keep all the points and articles which in these aforesaid orders are continued, as by the same orders thereof made more plainly doth and may appear. And, finally, if the said Master or Usher shall manifestly neglect or break any of the said orders, being thereof twice admonished by the said Master and Wardens, governors aforesaid, and notwithstanding continue the breach thereof, that then it shall be lawful to the said Master and Wardens, governors aforesaid, to expel and put out the party so offending and to place another able man in his room or office.

THESE ARTICLES perused, approved, and subscribed to by the most Reverend Father in God, Matthew, Archbishop of Canterbury, Primate of all England and Metropolitan, and by the Right Worshipful Alexander Nowell, Dean of the Cathedral Church of Saint Paul in London, the twelfth day of May, in the year of our Sovereign Lady Elizabeth of England, France, and Scotland, Queen Defender of the Faith, and so forth, the Sixth. *The Statutes subscribed by Archbishop Parker and Dean Nowell.*

(Signed)   MATTHEW CANTUAR.
ALEXANDER NOWELL.

The perusal of these Statutes was obtained by the Governors six years after the death of the Founder, and the formal request of the Master and Wardens of the Skinners' Company was made to Archbishop Parker, 7th May, 1564, as is shown by the following extract from the correspondence of Archbishop Parker, Letter CLX. (Parker MSS. C. C. Coll. Camb. CVIII. Art. 65. p. 415 Orig.)

"With all humbleness. It may please your good grace to understand, that where one Sir Andrew Judd, late knight and alderman of the city of London, did appoint your humble beseechers, the Master and Wardens of the Company of Skinners in London, governors of a certain grammar school in the town of Tunbridge in the county of Kent, *Sir Andrew Judde having founded a Grammar school at Tonbridge, and ap-*

58 TONBRIDGE SCHOOL.

pointed the Skinners' Company governors,

the Court of Wards ordered them to stand to such rules for its government as the archbishop and dean Nowell should appoint. Proposed statutes are therefore submitted to them.

by the said Sir Andrew builded and erected, yet through sundry occasions much trouble hath for these four or five years happened to the said Governors for the defence thereof in the Queen's Majesty's Court of Wards and Liveries; and in quieting thereof it is thus ordered by the master and council of the said Court of Wards and Liveries, that the said Governors shall stand bound in a thousand marks to stand to the good order of your Grace and Mr. Nowell, the Dean of Paul's, for the appointing of the rules and orders for the government of the said school and scholars there: and for the finishing thereof, there are certain orders written and perused by the said right worshipful master, Dean of Paul's, as by his handwriting may appear, beseeching your Grace to peruse the same according to your godly wisdom, and upon the allowing thereof to subscribe the same with your Grace's hand, that thereby your humble beseechers may come to quietness. And thus your humble beseechers shall daily pray to God for the prosperous estate of your Grace in honour long to continue. From London the seventh day of May, 1564. Your most humble beseechers,

    by me WYLLM. FLETCHER.
    by me THOMAS BANNESTER.
    by me THOMAS ALLEN.
    by me THOMAS STARKY.
    by me JHON METCAWFFE.

"To the Right Honourable Lord, the Lord Archbishop's Grace of Canterbury, be this delivered."

The "orders" for Tonbridge School are preserved in the article immediately preceding this letter (Parker MS.

CVIII. 64.) They exhibit a variety of alterations and additions both in the handwriting of Nowell, to whom they were first submitted, and also in that of Parker. At the end of them are the autograph subscriptions of the Dean and Archbishop, and also a memorandum written by the Archbishop. They are as follows :—

"These articles, touching the School at Tunbridge, I have perused, and do like them well.

"ALEXANDER NOWELL."

As an instance of Dean Nowell's alterations, one of the original rules was that no "remedy for playe" should be allowed "above ffower tymes in the yere." The Dean wrote in the margin, "Leave to play once a weeke may well be borne with." In the rules of St. Paul's School drawn up by Dean Colet, he says, "I will they use no cock-figtinge, nor rydinge about of victorye, nor disputing at Saint Bartholomewe, which is but foolish babbling, and lusse of time. I will also that they shall have no *remedyes*. If the maister grantith any remedyes he shall forfeit xls. totiens quotiens except the Kyng or an Archbishopp, or a Bishop present in his own person in the Scole desire it[1]." The word "remedy" was also used in this sense at Winchester[2] and Westminster.

"Remedies."

In 1693 the privileges of the foundationers (called in these Statutes the "first class") were disputed, and again in 1764; on which last occasion, Sir F. Norton and Sir W. Blackstone argued the case. In 1825 the matter was settled, and a ten miles' radius, exclusive of the county of Sussex, from Tonbridge Church was fixed as a limit to the freedom of the School; a decision which remains in force to the present day.

[1] Knight's Life of Colet, ed. 1724, p. 362.   [2] Vide page 65.

THE ORIGINAL BUILDING

The old School building.

THE old School [1], pulled down in 1863 to make room for the present one, was built of Kentish sandstone from the neighbouring quarries. Sandstone has the peculiar property of becoming harder by age, instead of crumbling away: so while the interior beams and woodwork of the old School had become entirely rotten, the original outside walls were hard and firm, except in one or two places in the front, where slight cracks had appeared. The print on the opposite page shows Sir Andrew Judde's building when the first Head Master was appointed in 1558, but the low building on the left hand is a Library added about 1760, by the Rev. J. Cawthorn [2], one of the Head Masters, conjointly with the Skinners' Company. The length in front was 160 feet, and the breadth corresponded exactly to the breadth

And description of it.

[1] I have a copy of several old architectural plans of the School which bear no date. They show alterations and additions at the back of the School, but, otherwise, are of little importance. My thanks are due to Mr. Edward Burnell, the architect of the present School and a member of the Skinner's Company, for the loan of these plans.—S. R.

[2] Vide page 119.

THE ORIGINAL BUILDING

of the Old Upper School, about 25 feet: thus the original building had the shape of a rectangular parallelogram. The Head Master's house was on the left side or south end and next to the Library; the Second Master's on the right side or north end: the former about 45, and the latter about 26 feet in length. The old "Upper School," the only School-room then existing, and about 40 feet long, was between the two Masters' houses. The raised end, where the fourth form used to sit in class, and where the bell-rope used to hang down, mended the place of the partition wall of the Second Master's house. This internal arrangement of the School continued for more than two hundred and fifty years, till Judde House, the present residence and boarding-house belonging to the Second Master, was built. Then the School-room was lengthened to the size it was (viz. 55 feet by 25 feet) at the time of its demolition in 1863, by the addition of part of the original Second Master's house. As it is supposed that there were not more than about twenty or thirty boys at the School for some time after its foundation, it is natural that the building should not have received any considerable addition for many years. The inscription which is placed over the Head Master's present front door, was removed from the front door of the School building lately pulled down. Yet this was not its original position. It formerly was over a window—once the Head Master's door—on the left hand side (facing the building) of the front door of the old School. The walls, when stripped in 1863 of their plaster and woodwork on the inside, showed these alterations plainly, as well as the door,

_{The inscription over the front door was removed.}

---

[1] For mention of the brick chimney richly moulded in front of the building, vide Parker's Domestic Architecture, vol. iii. p. 119.

afterwards filled up with rubble and bricks, of the Second Master's former house.

The inscription. The inscription is now built into the wall over Dr. Welldon's front door, and for its quaintness and simplicity deserves transcription :—

THIS · SHOLE · MADE · BI · SIR ·
ANDRO · IWDE · KNIGHT · AND ·
GEVIN · TO · THE · COMPANE ·
OF · SKIÑERS · AÑO · 1553.

The different alterations in the building connected with the School will be alluded to under the Head Masters in whose time they were made.

THE OLD ROUTINE OF SCHOOL WORK

WHEN the School was first opened under the care of the Rev. John Proctour, the daily routine and working of it was something of this sort. The Head Master was to be, at least, a Master of Arts, chosen by the Skinners' Company on account of his learning and "dexterity in teaching." His religion was to be "that now set forth by public authority" (Protestant). The Master appointed the Usher, the former receiving twenty pounds, and the latter eight pounds a year; and the number of boarders taken by the Master might not exceed twelve, and by the Usher, eight, unless the Governours saw fit to increase these numbers. Neither of them could be absent from the School (excepting during the holidays) for more than twenty days in the year, and that only for urgent reasons. No boy could be admitted without the Master having previously examined him and proved him able to write perfectly English

The University standing of the Head Master

Admission of boys to the School.

and Latin, nor might any one be more than five years in learning his grammar. The Master licensed houses for the boys to board at in the town; and without his leave, no house could be opened to receive scholars. When a boy entered the School, there was a "Common Box" into which he deposited sixpence for the use of books, and into which all fines for absences, extra remedies and books were to be paid. The sketch below may give some idea of one of these "Common Boxes." The original of this sketch is in Dr. Welldon's possession; it is made of iron with a heavy handle, and has the arms of the Skinners' Company on two of its sides.

Licensing of boarding houses.

THE "COMMON BOX."

The Common Box.

It is probable that this box continued in ordinary use till nearly the end of the last century. If a boy was absent without leave, he did not get an imposition or a flogging, as his probable fate would be now-a-days, but he paid a fine of a penny for each day's absence. A register was kept with the name of every boy in the School on it; and this register was, and is now, annually inspected by the Governours.

At seven o'clock in the morning there was a general muster in the School-room for prayers. Work then began and continued till eleven o'clock: in the afternoon, it lasted from one till five. Latin was to be spoken by the Masters to those who could understand it, and the whole School, twice a month, was examined personally by the Head Master, as it is to this day. Once a fortnight was the limit to extra holidays, which were called *Remedies*[1]—a very good name, the restoration of which is worth the consideration of the Masters and boys of the present generation. But if a "worshipful" person, that is, a man of eminence or rank, was present in the School, and asked for a "Remedy," provided such a thing did not happen more than once in the same week, it was allowed to be granted. But if it happened more than once in the same week, the "offender," that is to say, the second worshipful person, had to pay into the "Common Box" a fine of three shillings and fourpence[2].

School hours,

And work.

Extra holidays might be granted.

---

[1] Remedy. The same name is still used at Winchester for some holidays. It is derived most probably from *remedium (laboris)*. "A kind of mitigated holiday, of which there was always one, and generally two a week. The boys went into school twice in the course of the day for an hour, but no master was present. A Remedy was not a matter of course, but the Head Master was always asked by the Præfect of Hall to give one while he was walking up and down 'Sands' (the pavement of quadrangle under chapel windows) before morning chapel: if he intended to grant the request, he gave to the suppliant a ring engraved with the words, '*Commendat rarior usus*.' This ring he wore till the following day, and returned to the Head Master at Middle school."—School-Life at Winchester College, p. 229. Vide also p. 61.

[2] An entry in a MS. in the School Library proves the continuance to a late date of this custom: "Rev. N. Andrews, 1l. 1s. for a holiday, Dec. 2, 1796."

All the boys must attend church.

On Sunday morning the boys with prayer books in Latin or English went to the Parish Church, accompanied by at least one Master, whose duty it was to call to account on Monday mornings the absentees and those who came late, as prescribed by the Statutes. In these arrangements

The difference between the present and original arrangements of the work.

there seem to be but few points of importance that differ from those of the present day. The aggregate of the hours of work were about the same length, if so long, as at the present day; but the manner of dividing them into two long stretches is opposed to our idea that the mind of a boy will not readily or profitably stand the strain of several continuous hours' application.

Much stress was laid upon the excellent practice of speaking colloquially the dead languages; and the admittance of boys to the School must have been limited (so much so, indeed, as to debar the very people for whose benefit the School was originally founded from using its privileges), if the requirements of the Statutes were rigorously enforced. For, as a matter of fact, none of the boys that come to School from Tonbridge town and its neighbourhood can now, nor probably could then, "write and read perfectly English and Latin."

SKINNERS' DAY

"SKINNERS' DAY" is an institution as old as the School *The Annual* itself. The ceremony was once imposing and is still *Visitation day.* interesting. It was a great thing for Tonbridge when the members of a large city Company, after posting down from London, made a triumphal entry into the town, to visit the School; and having awarded the prizes and exhibitions, and distributed alms to the poor of the townspeople, they returned to London till the following summer saw them again delight the hearts of the boys and the neighbourhood with the sight of the imposing array of four-horse carriages drawn up at the School entrance.

Up to the year 1798 the Governours visited the School, riding on horseback, and encamped on Sevenoaks Common to take their breakfast. After that date they posted, two or three in a chaise, and met for breakfast at the "White Hart," Sevenoaks; at Hildenborough, about a mile and a half from Tonbridge, they were welcomed with a chime from some musical blacksmiths, who stood in a circle bowing in turn as they struck each a note on their ploughshares with a small hammer. During their last stage from Sevenoaks to Tonbridge, the Governours used to distribute *largess* in the form of coppers to the villagers who turned out to see them; and as they neared the School, where they arrived about twelve o'clock, some of the boys used to go to meet them, racing back by the side of the post-chaises to see their arrival at the School gates, and hear the Latin address delivered by the head boy, and the reply of the Examiner.

The decoration of the High Street.

There is an old custom, absurd were it not for its antiquity, which commands respect, of lining the High Street of the town with branches of birch; what was the origin of this happy and highly suggestive idea is unknown.

The first or second day after May Day was formerly fixed for "Skinners' Day," and the proceedings were as follows:

The Disputations.

Disputations on questions previously provided by the Head Master were publicly held in the School-room, before the Masters and Wardens of the Company and an audience of any one who chose to attend. These began about one o'clock, and lasted for an hour. By the special request of the Head Master, the Vicar of Tonbridge and other "learned men" were present to aid in deciding the merit of the disputants. A few of these dialogues of a comparatively late date will be found at the end of this book. Three prizes were given:

The prizes.

the first was a pen of "silver whole guilt," to cost two shillings and sixpence; the second, a pen of "silver parcell guilt," to cost two shillings; and the third, "a pen of silver," to cost twenty pence. There was no Examiner appointed at first: probably Sir Thomas Smythe introduced one during his lifetime, as Gataker preached before him at one of the

Company's visitations. When these prizes had been distributed, every one went to the church in a procession of two and two; last in order, immediately after the Master and Usher of the School, came the three prize-holders, wearing on their heads garlands of flowers. They were placed in a conspicuous position in the church, where appropriate psalms and hymns, with a prayer for the Founder and the reigning Sovereign, were repeated.

The famous John Evelyn, the author of Sylva, a treatise on forest trees, for which he has often been known by the name of the Sylvan Evelyn, writes in his published Diary (vol. i. p. 576) under the year 1665, during the Head Mastership of Dr. Wase, "April 28—I went to Tunbridge, to see a solemn exercise at the Free Schoole there." The "Bellum Grammaticale[1]," edited by the Rev. Richard Spencer, was a well-known book in its time, and is a specimen of the Latin plays in use at the time. *(John Evelyn. One of the original plays.)*

In Dr. Thomas Knox's time (about 1830), the day before the examination of the School, that is, Monday, used to be called "flower day." This name arose from the custom of the head boys collecting from their friends in the neighbourhood flowers to decorate the town and the School-room, and to make the garlands that each of the three head boys wore on their heads or carried in their hands as they went to church on "Skinners' Day." These garlands were in a tall conical shape, in fact, very much like fool's-caps. Dr. Thomas Knox used to give a grand ball in the evening in the library, and the three head boys, winners of the garlands, selected each his lady-love, and led off the dance at the opening of the ball. *("Flower day" in Dr. Knox's time. The garlands used to be worn by the head boys.)*

[1] Vide page 142.

The present Skinners' Day.

The present "Skinners' Day" differs in details only from the original one; the object is the same, namely, the personal inspection of the School by the Governours, but the day is welcomed by all at School as a sign of the close of the term. After a "call over" of the whole School about nine o'clock on the morning of the first day, all the boys assemble in front of the School entrance to await the arrival of the Governours, who drive up in carriages attended by the Examiner. A Latin speech is then delivered at the front door by the head boy, who enumerates the chief events of the past year connected with the School, the Examiner replying also in Latin. After entering, the Examiner reads out the mottoes of the successful prize compositions. The *vivâ voce* examination of the lowest form then commences in the large School-room, which is thrown open to any one who wishes to be present, and continues throughout the day till seven o'clock, when there is a service in the Chapel. Shortly after nine o'clock on the next morning the Governours and the School attend a special service at the Parish Church. This service used formerly to be held at the end of the day instead of at the commencement. On returning to the School, the Clerk of the Skinners' Company calls over the whole School by Christian and surname in order of seniority by time, and reads out the Statutes. The competitors for exhibitions then give in their names, and are examined *vivâ voce*. Afterwards the prizes, including the three pens, are awarded by the Master of the Company in the presence of the Governours, the Examiner, the Masters, and a considerable number of visitors, and selections from the prize compositions are read from a raised dais by the respective winners of the

The Orat. Congrat.

The examination.

The prizes.

prizes. This terminates the proceedings and closes the term; the boys disperse for the Midsummer holidays, and the Governours, who during their stay have inspected the School and distributed their annual gifts in the Parish Church to the poor of the town, invite the Masters and the head boy to dinner in the evening.

The following Latin prayers were, for many years, used upon the morning of the second day of the two "Skinners' Days." They were to be read every morning for a fortnight before "Skinners' Day," in order to accustom the boys to follow the prayers and repeat the responses. Latterly, however, they were only used for a day or two before "Skinners' Day;" and, in 1868, when the service in the Parish Church on the second day was altered from the afternoon to the morning, they were discontinued altogether.

LATINÆ PRECES.

M. Laudemus corde et ore Dominum.
N. Laudemus nomen Domini.
M. Qui noctis tenebras dispulit.
N. Et lucem nobis reddidit.

The Latin Prayers.

OREMUS.

Pater noster, qui es in cœlis, sanctificetur nomen tuum; Adveniat regnum tuum; Fiat voluntas tua, sicut in cœlo, sic et in terrâ. Panem nostrum quotidianum da nobis hodie. Et remitte nobis debita nostra, sicut et nos remittimus debitoribus nostris. Et ne nos inducas in tentationem, sed libera nos à malo; Quia tuum est regnum, potentia, et gloria in sæcula sæculorum. *Amen.*

The Latin Prayers.

Prayers for the Founder and Sir Thomas Smythe.

Æterne Deus, à quo solo omne bonum consilium, omnis bona cogitatio procedit, gratias tibi maximas agimus, quòd viris optimis, et Andreæ Judd, militi, Scholam hanc piè instituendi, magnoque sumptu suo exstruendi et dotandi; et quòd Thomæ Smythe, militi, eam nec minore sumptu suo augendi et in perpetuum faciendi consilium inspirasti; Teque suppliciter oramus, ut eam à calamitate omni tuearis; et Ecclesiæ, regnoque tuo utilem semper facias; et ut nos cum omni diligentiâ eò contendamus quò pii illi nos pervenire voluerunt, ut benè pièque eruditi Ecclesiæ tuæ et Reipublicæ tandem utiles evadamus, per Jesum Christum, Dominum nostrum. *Amen.*

Clementissime Pater coelestis, qui coelum et terras et quæ in iis sunt omnia summâ sapientiâ condidisti; eademque providentiâ tuâ perpetuò regis et conservas,—concede, quæsumus, quemadmodùm optimi illi, Andreas Judd, et Thomas Smythe, milites, spectatâ societatis Pellionum fide et providentiâ freti, eorum curæ hanc Scholam commiserunt,—ut et ipsi, fidei suæ his defunctis debitæ semper memores, Scholam hanc diligentèr curent et tueantur; tandemque, post hujus vitæ cursum honestè confectum, æternum fidelissimæ illius procurationis suæ præmium in coelis consequantur, per Jesum Christum, Dominum nostrum. *Amen.*

Æterne Deus, Pater Domini ac Salvatoris nostri, Jesu Christi—qui parentes nobis, præceptores, amicosque concessisti, ut nostræ ætati res necessarias subministrarent,—eam in bonis literis et disciplinis educarent,—consilio denique et monitis errantem in viam revocarent,—majestatem tuam suppliciter oramus, pro parentibus filii obsequentes, pro præceptoribus discipuli officiosi, pro amicis pueri ingenui; ut eos omnes tuâ misericordiâ digneris, quò et præceptores literarii suo erga te, in nobis erudiendis, officio defungantur,—parentes nostri præceptorum diligentiæ in nobis educandis pari studio respondeant, et amici nostri pro facultate suâ, nostræ infirmitati consulant:—ut, cùm tandem reddenda erit nostræ educationis, correctionisque ratio, cum gaudio eam reddant; et suæ erga nos pietatis studiique prœmium æternum consequantur, per Jesum Christum, Dominum nostrum. *Amen.* The Latin Prayers.

Domine Pater, cœli ac terræ effector, qui liberaliter tribuis sapientiam omnibus, eam à te cum fiduciâ petentibus,—Exorna, quæsumus, ingeniorum nostrum bonitatem, quam, cum cæteris naturæ viribus, nobis infudisti, lumine divinæ gratiæ tuæ, ut non modo quæ ad cognoscendum te, et Salvatorem nostrum, Dominum Jesum Christum, valeant intelligamus; sed etiam tota mente et voluntate prosequamur; et indies benignitate tuâ tum doctrinâ tum pietate proficiamus; ut, qui efficis omnia in omnibus, in nobis resplendescere dona tua facias ad gloriam sempiternam immortalis majestatis tuæ, per Jesum Christum, Dominum nostrum. *Amen.*

M. Κύριε ἐλέησον.

N. Χριστὲ ἐλέησον.

M. Notam fac nobis viam tuam, Domine.

N. Spiritus tuus bonus nos ducat.

M. Pellat ex animis nostris cogitationes malas.

N. Ut attenti simus sermonibus disciplinæ.

M. Gloria Patri, et Filio, et Spiritui Sancto.

N. Sicut erat in principio, nunc est, et semper erit, in sæcula sæculorum. *Amen.*

VISITORS

Uncertainty as to the Visitors was settled after a time.

SOME doubt was for a long time felt as to who were legally the Visitors of the School, the Skinners' Company having always acted as such. By the Founder, "Collegium Omnium Sanctorum" is named, but as no college at Oxford or Cambridge was ever styled by that title, it was decided before the Lord Chancellor that All Souls', Oxford, was meant, and that the Warden and Fellows of that College are the Visitors proper. It is certain that their opinion may be taken as a reference in matters of importance (which has, however, been rarely done), while they have also in their hands the nomination of the annual Examiner, who has a fee of thirty guineas, and whose qualification is, that he must be a Master of Arts of Oxford or Cambridge, of not less than seven years' standing.

The exercise of their functions is seldom called for.

The Visitors were to exercise a

The Visitors' duties, as regards the School, were accurately expressed for them in the Founder's will, thus: to "See and consider whether the School Master and Usher do their duties towards the scholars, in teaching them virtue and learning; and whether the scholars do of their part use themselves virtuous and studious, and whether they do observe and keep the orders and rules of my free School or not; and I will that the Master and Wardens in their visitation shall take heed that if any of the rules or orders in my School shall fortune to be broken either by the Master and the Usher, or by any of the scholars, that then the same may be forthwith reformed and amended, according to their good directions and as my special trust and confidence in them."

<small>general supervision over the state of the School.</small>

A LIST OF THE HEAD MASTERS OF THE SCHOOL

FROM ITS FOUNDATION TO THE PRESENT TIME

DATE.	NAME.	PAGE.
1558—1578.	Rev. John Proctour, M.A.	77— 83
1578—1588.	Rev. John Stockwood, M.A.	84— 92
1588—	Rev. William Hatch, M.A.	93
1640.	Rev. Michael Jenkins, M.A.	93
1640—1647.	Rev. Thomas Horne, D.D.	94— 96
1647—1657.	Rev. Nicholas Grey, D.D.	97— 98
1657—1661.	Rev. John Goad, B.D.	99—102
1661—1680.	Rev. Christopher Wase, B.D.	103—108
1680—1714.	Rev. Thomas Roots, M.A.	109—111
1714—1743.	Rev. Richard Spencer, M.A.	112—115
1743—1761.	Rev. James Cawthorn, M.A.	116—121
1761—1770.	Rev. Johnson Towers, M.A.	122—123
1770—1778.	Rev. Vicesimus Knox, LL.B.	124—125
1778—1812.	Rev. Vicesimus Knox, D.D.	126—145
1812—1843.	Rev. Thomas Knox, D.D.	146—189
1843	Rev. James Ind Welldon, D.C.L.	190—228

JOHN PROCTOUR, M.A.

1558—1578

JOHN PROCTOUR, M.A., was appointed the First _{Elected} Master of the School in 1558, and was probably _{probably by the} elected by Sir Andrew Judde himself, since the date of the _{Founder.} Founder's death and of Proctour's election was nearly the same.

John Proctour was born in Somersetshire, was a scholar _{His education} in 1536 of Corpus Christi College, Oxford, and took his degree of B.A. in 1540, and of M.A. in 1544. About this time he became a Fellow of All Souls' College, where a brother of Sir Andrew Judde's was also a Fellow. He wrote "The Historie of Wyate's Rebellion, with the order _{And literary} and maner of resisting the same; whereunto at the ende _{works.} is added, an earnest conference with the degenerate and sedicious rebelles for the serche of the cause of their daily disorder. Made and compyled by John Proctour, published January, 1555." 16mo.¹

His short history a valuable work.

This book, of which Holinshed also made use in the compilation of his Chronicles, has a special value for the reason which Bishop Nicholson gives in his English Historical Library² : " A slender account of Wyatt's Rebellion was sent out by John Proctor of Tunbridge, who (for any thing I have yet learned) must be looked upon as the only particular historian of this reign."

He wrote also two other works : " The Fall of the late Arian, 1549," in which he combats, at length, the Arian heretical principles, and " The Way Home to Christ, and Truths leading from Anti-Christ and Errour, made and set fourth in the Latine Tongue, by that famous and great Clerk Vincent, Frenchman born, above 1100 years past, for the comfort of all true Christian men, 1546." These were

The reasons for suspecting him of an inclination to the Church of Rome are strong.

dedicated to Queen Mary, and hence arises the reason for supposing him to have had a leaning to the Roman Catholics. Either his desire for favour with the party in power influenced his religion more than it should have done, or else he was at heart a Papist.

We hear nothing of John Proctour after 1580; it is probable, therefore, that he either left the School, or died, being still Head Master, in that year.

Dr. Bliss, Athen. Oxon. I. p. 235, adds to the above, that Newcourt, in his Repertorium Ecclesiasticum, fol. 1708, p. 176, supposes this John Proctour to have been the Proctour who was presented to the Rectory of St. Andrew, Holborn, in March 13, 1578, who died there in 1584. Dr.

---

[1] Dr. Welldon has a copy of this rare little work. See Lowndes' Bibliographer's Manual, 1864, vol. iii. pp. 1978, 1979.
[2] Preface, Part II. p. 46.

Bliss, however, thinks that this must be an error on Newcourt's part, as Standish, in his "Treatise against the Translation of the Bible into the Vulgar Language," commends Proctour, which he would not have done had he not been a rigid Papist. Dr. Bliss holds that there is no doubt that Proctour was a Papist from the translation of the Tract cited above, viz. "The Way Home to Christ."

Two men of note were educated under Proctour, viz. Robert Heath and Francis Thynne.

ROBERT HEATH[1] began his education under the First, and finished his School career under the Second Head Master. In an autobiography, written shortly before his death, Heath says, "Uppon the 20th day of May, in the year 1575, I was borne at Brastid, in Kent, of Robert Heath, Gent., my father, and Jane, his wife, my mother." As early as fourteen years old he left Tonbridge, and went to St. John's College, Cambridge, for three years. He then went to Clifford's Inn for a year, and when eighteen, removed to the Inner Temple for ten years, and was called to the bar in 1603. Four years after he was appointed Reader of Clifford's Inn, which office he held for two years while practising at the Bar. In 1610 he became a Bencher in the Inner Temple, was Reader there in 1611, and Treasurer in 1625. The favourite Buckingham lent him his valuable support, and by this means Heath was elected Recorder of London, and from 1618 to 1621 was Solicitor-General[2].

His autobiography.

His professional success.

The year of his election to the Recordership of London, the Aldermen presented him out of "especial love and

---

[1] Foss's Lives of the Judges, vol. ii. p. 320.

[2] Campbell's Lives of the Chief Justices, vol. i. ch. 2.

favour " with 100*l*., two hogsheads of claret, and one pipe of canary, and on his resigning the office of Treasurer to take that of Solicitor-General, he was chosen Member of Parliament for the citizens of London. He frequently took part in the debates, and by his exertions in favour of the King (James I.) he was knighted, and retained in his office till the end of the reign. His opinions were very peculiar, and he supported them with great learning and ability. It was his maxim that "the King can do no wrong," and he several times refused a seat in the House of Commons, calling it "only fit for a pitiful Puritan or a pretending patriot."

<small>His opinions were in favour of the King, who frequently made use of his able services.</small>

In 1625, on the accession of Charles I., Heath became Attorney-General, and in the following year was engaged by the King and the Duke of Buckingham to charge the Earl of Bristol with high treason, in order to invalidate that nobleman's irrefutable evidence against Buckingham. The unpleasant duty of opposing, in 1627, the release of the Knights, who, refusing to contribute to Charles's forced loan, had been arbitrarily imprisoned, was committed to him. In this contest Heath was confronted with Sir Edward Coke, Littleton, Noy, and Selden. Against such men he acquitted himself with no loss of reputation, though he failed to gain his invidious cause. At the violent termination of Charles's Parliament, in May, 1629, Sir Robert Heath played a prominent part in the imprisonment of the Members who, by force detained the Speaker in his chair, in order to prolong the Session till some business obnoxious to the King had been transacted. In October, 1631, he was elevated to the rank of Chief Justice of the Common Pleas, and two years later he opposed Archbishop Laud in the Star Chamber. In 1634 he was summarily dismissed from office without any cause being assigned. Just at this time Banks, on the death of Noy, became Attorney-General, and Finch succeeded Heath. The following lines were stuck up on the gates of Westminster Hall, joking on these changes of office:— *His dismissal from office.*

> "Noy's flood is gone,
> The Banks appear,
> Heath is shorn down,
> And Finch sings there."

Hacket says, in his account of the prosecution of Archbishop Williams by Laud, "Sir Robert Heath was displaced, and for no misdemeanour proved; but it was to bring in a successor who was more forward to undo Lincoln than ever Lord Heath was to preserve him." Wood[1] says that he was removed from the Chief Justiceship for bribery, but Heath's own words are, "At the end of three years, I was on a sudden discharged of that place of Chief Justice, no cause being then or at any other time said and showed for my removal."

However, he renewed practice at the Bar as Junior Serjeant in the same court in which he had just been Chief Justice; in two years he became King's Serjeant, and in 1641 was made a Judge of the King's Bench. He became D.C.L. of Oxford in A.D. 1643, and was also then raised to the Chief Justiceship of the King's Bench. He never, however, exercised the duties of this office in Westminster Hall, as the House of Commons, in consequence of his adherence to the King during the Civil Wars, passed an *His wonderful energy in beginning life afresh.*

---

[1] Athenæ Oxonienses, vol. ii. p. 584.

ordinance against him and four others "as though they were dead:" they gave him the choice of "either to exile himself into a foreign country, or run the hazard of further danger. His estates were sequestered, but in 1663 were recovered by his son. Sir Robert Heath retired as an exile to France, and, while there, he wrote his own memoir and a *jeu d'esprit* on the twenty-four links of the collar of S. S.[1]—each link representing some juridical attribute beginning with the letter S. There are twenty-four words beginning with this letter. This collar is now in the possession of the family of Lord Willoughby de Broke, one of whose ancestors a relation of Sir Robert Heath had married.

His death took place at Calais, August 30, 1649; and Brastid Church, Kent, contains his monument. Two books were published some years after his death, which may be found in the British Museum and the Bodleian Library at Oxford. One is "Maxims and Rules of Pleading, from the MS. of Sir Robert Heath," the other, "A Collection of Precedents by Bill and Answer, &c., for more than 30 years past;" both are law books published at London in 1694, the latter being probably written during his lifetime.

FRANCIS THYNNE[2], born in Kent about A.D. 1545, was descended from Ralp de Boteville, whose eldest son got nicknamed *Thom at the Inne*, and so his descendants assumed the name of Thynne. His father was Master of the Household to Henry VIII.

Francis Thynne himself, after having been educated "in grammaticals," went to Magdalen College, Oxford, and from thence to Lincoln's Inn. He was a renowned anti-

---

[1] Notes and Queries, vol. x. p. 557. [2] Hearne's Collection of Curious Discourses.

quary and a deeply read scholar, and very learned in the study of heraldry and pedigrees. He was made Blanche Lyon Poursuivant; and in 1602, when fifty-seven years of age, he was with great ceremony created Lancaster Herald, both offices in the College of Arms. His fame was also drawn from another source; for about 1586 he greatly helped Holinshed in the compilation of his Chronicles, even more so than has been generally supposed, since many of his writings in it were suppressed. The reasons are given at length in Hearne's "Collection of Curious Discourses," where a list of the books he wrote (almost all on antiquarian subjects) will be found.

He is believed to have died about 1608, at the age of sixty-three.

And became a great antiquarian.

His aid to Holinshed was considerable.

JOHN STOCKWOOD, M.A.

1578—1588

THE Rev. John Stockwood succeeded Proctour about 1578. He was a very eminent scholar in his day, and a noted grammarian. It is probable that he was Master for not more than ten years, since in 1589 he calls himself "Minister and Preacher at Tunbridge," and considered it a promotion to give up his Mastership for the sake of becoming the Vicar of the place.

<small>A great grammatical scholar.</small>

Stockwood's books were published in the following order :—

<small>His literary works.</small>

1. "A short and learned Treatise of the Plague, written in Latin by the famous and worthy Divine, Theodore Beza Vegelian, and newly turned into English by John Stockwood, Schoolemaister of Tunbridge, 1680."

2. "A short Catechisme for House holders, with prayers to the same adjoygning. Hereunto are added, under the aunswer unto everie question, the prouves of Scripture for everie point of the said Catechisme. Gathered by John

Stockwood, Schoolemaister of Tunbridge, according as they were noted in the Margin by the first authors." The text is from Psalm xxxiv. 2; the date, Sept. 15, 1583; and the dedication is to John Hart, Alderman of London. His literary works.

3. "A very fruitfull and necessarye Sermon of the most lamentable destruction of Jerusalem," with the text from Luke xiii. 3. "Unless yee repent, yee shall all perish in like manner," published 1584.

4. "A verie godlie and profitable Sermon of the necessary properties and office of a good Magistrate." Deuteronomy xviii. 26; published 1584. It is addressed "to the worshipful Maiors, Bayliffs, Jurates, and Freemen of Her Maiestie's Cinque Ports and lymes of the same."

The following extract from it shows the quaint style of writing made use of in those times:—

"A covetous magistrate," says he, "maketh under officers unto him, Rapax, Capax, Tenax. Yea, so as he may gain by them, he careth not whether they be drunkards," &c. These three words, Rapax, Capax, Tenax, he translates in a marginal note by "Snatch, Catch, Holdfast." An extract from one of them.

5. "A Bartholomew Fairing[1] for Parentes, to bestow upon their sonnes and daughters, and for one friend to give to another, shewing that children are not to marie, without the consent of their parentes, in whose power and choise it lieth to provide wives and husbandes for their sonnes and daughters. Wherein is sufficiently proved, what in this point is the office of the fathers, and in like manner declared the part and duty of all obedient children. By John Stockwood, Minister and Preacher of Tunbridge, 1589."

The book is dedicated "To the Right Worshipful,

---

[1] Lowndes's Bibliographer's Manual, 1864, vol. iii. p. 2520.

Mr. Thomas Skeuington of Skeuington, Esquire, at the present High Sheriffe of Leicestershire, and one of Her Maiestie's Trustees of the Peace there:—John Stockwood, Minister and Preacher of the Worde of God at Tunbridge in Kent, wisheth all felicitie of mind and bodie, through Jesus Christ, our most merciful Redeemer." The author proceeds in his preface to explain the reason of the title in these words: "The time falling out so fitlie with the finishing of this worke and the publishing of the same, I have given unto it the name of Bartholomew Fairing, the rather by the novelty of the title to drawe on the multitude of people that now, out of all places of our county repaire unto the citie to the better beholding and consideration of the matter contained in this Treatise." This, of course, refers to the annual Fair, which, till a few years ago, used to be held in Smithfield on St. Bartholomew's Day, when enormous crowds were assembled in and about London.

6. It was after the publication of these books that Stockwood's distinguished qualities as a grammarian began to become known, by his "First Grammar of the English Language: a plain and easy laying open of the meaning and the understanding of the Rules of Construction in the English Accidence, appointed by authoritie to be taught in all Schooles of Her Maiestie's dominions, for the great use and benefit of yooung beginners, by John Stockwood, sometime School maister of Tunbridge." The dedicatory letter bears the date of November 16, 1590, and is addressed to the "Master William Lewin, Doctor of both Lawes, Justice of the Peace," &c.; the preface "to the friendlie Reader" ends with "from my studie at Tunbridge, 14 of Jan., 1588, thy poore brother in Christ unfeinedlie tending thy good

His English Grammar.

wherein he may." The plan of this Grammar is by question and answer, of simple and ingenious contrivance.

After the preface, the following piece of poetry welcomes the infant mind that is destined to learn the Grammar. *The address to the reader.*

THE BOOKE TO THE
Yoong Punies and Petits [1]
of the Grammar Schoole.

"When painfull Master had no time
   In plainest sort your rules to teach;
Or clubbish fellows shall refuse
   Their friendly helpe heerin to reach;
Bicause you come with emptie hand
   And profer not thrice welcome fee,
(Which thing some schollars much desire)
   Then boldly make resort to me,
I will you helpe, make proofe who list,
   And set you downe the easie way,
Youre english rules to understand
   Their meaning open for to lay.
For each example to his rule,
   I teach you aptly how to fit;
Thus you may laugh where others cry
   When up they go, for missing it.
Now, as for fee I none do crave,
   I aske no other recompence,
The paine is mine, the profit thine
   Vsing this booke with diligence."

---

[1] At Westminster School, founded nearly about the same time as Tonbridge, the lowest form of all used to be called the "Petty," evidently implying that it contained the smallest boys. The name is now almost obsolete, but was well known at Westminster thirty years ago.

In 1597, there appeared in London " Progymnasia Scholasticum, hoc est, Epigrammatum Græcorum ex Anthologia selectorum ab H. Stephano, operâ et industriâ Joh. Stockwoodi, Scholæ Tunbridgiensis olim Ludi-Magistri," dedicated to Robert " Deuorax," Earl of Essex. Stockwood wrote a great many epigrams in this on various subjects, such as these three :—

" Hic pede mancus erat sed et alter lumine luscus,
  Præstat et alternas pars sibi quæque vices.
Namque humeris mancum portabat cæcus, eundem
  Claudus sed stabili dirigit ille gradus.
En sic naturæ compensat uterque necesse
  Mutui et officii dulce levamen erat."

" Primam qui sepelit sponsam quæsitque secundam,
  Insano dignus qui pereat pelago."

" Qui semel expertus connubia, vultque secunda,
  Quis dolet infido si cadat ille salo."

His Latin Grammar.   Stockwood's second grammatical work was written about nine years after his first. It was a most successful book, and reached five or six editions. The dedication is dated 1606. Several "old boys" have written complimentary verses in the preface; and Dr. Grant, the then Head Master of Westminster School, prefixed eight lines of Latin Poetry to it, acknowledging his respect for the talents, and esteem for the character of Stockwood.

This is the title of the work :—

" Disputatiuncularum Grammaticalium Libellus ad puerorum in Scholis trivialibus exacuenda ingenia primum excogitatus... operâ et industriâ Johannis Stockwoodi Scholæ Tunbridgiensis olim Ludi-Magistri."—Ed. 4to. 1619. *His Latin Grammar.*

"Sum novus; ecce novo redeo vestitus amictu;
Auctior et multo quam prius ante fui."

The dedication is to "D. Gulielmo Sydleio, militi... patrono doctissimo," &c., a friend whom the author praises for his liberality to men of letters in distress. The heading to the verses written by old pupils runs as follows:—

"In Joan. Stockwoodi Scholæ Tunbridgiensis aliquando Ludi Magistri libellum puerilium disputatiuncularum, carmina gratulatoria suorum quorundam tunc temporis et loci discipulorum ad perpetuam erga eundem grati animi significationem." The first verses are composed by William Hatch, then Head Master of the School, and previously a pupil under Stockwood.

"Ad Joann. Stockwoodum quondam præceptorem suum, Guliel. Hatchius Scholæ Tunbrid. Archi-didascalus:— *The congratulatory verses of Rev. W. Hatch.*
 Optima grammaticæ teneris præcepta dedisti
  Præceptor pueris sedulus ipse tuis.
 Abreptus studiis postquam gravioribus esses
  Hisce nec exiguis rebus adesse vacat;
 Triste tuis χαίρειν dicis, cessasque docere,
  Sic tamen ut multis Gymnasiarcha sies.
 Præsentes paucos suavis tua lingua docebat,
  Absentes multos penna sonora docet.
 Sic quamvis taceas, tacitus tamen instruis omnes,
  Scilicet ipse taces, sed tua scripta docent.

AD BENEVOLUM LECTOREM.
 Quæ tibi munificâ Stockwoodus munera dextra *And the introduction to the public.*
  Largitur, gratâ percipe mente puer.

>   Exiguus mole est, ipso neque nomine major
>   Attamen est ingens nobilitate liber.
>   Grammaticæ videas multos præcepta fideli
>   Mente revolventes, utpote verba tenent.
>   Objicias si quid canonum si sensa requiras,
>   Hic labor, hoc opus est : inscia lingua silet.
>   Hic labor exiguus sensum docet, ardua solvit,
>   Dum διαζητήσει plurima discutiat.
>   Credas Grammaticæ bellum indicisse Poetas,
>   Hic lites dirimens, nil minus esse docet.
>   Insuper et linguas puerorum format, et illos,
>   Verba quibus discant disseruisse docet.
>   Hunc (studiose puer) studiosâ mente revolve,
>   Exiguus liber est, utilitate minor."

Gulielmus Dixonus, Oxoniensis, wrote two stanzas, of which this couplet ends one :—

> "Ergo celer tanti doctissima scripta magistri
>   Perlege, pande, para, dilige, disce, doce."

Gulielmus Altersoldus, Cantabr.; Robertus Porterus, Cantabr.; Petrus Frenchæus, Cantabr.; Johannes Turnerus, Oxon.; Fulcus Martialis, Cantabr.; Gulielmus Budgerius, Oxon.; Gulielmus Pyxus, Oxon., all wrote epigrams in praise of their former Master and his book. Thomas Thorpe, Oxon., wrote a short Ode on the annual Disputations held at the School. It is interesting as being the earliest mention of them, excepting in the Statutes, that is extant.

A specimen of the odes written in it by one of the Old Boys.

> "Descriptio disputationis Anniversariæ inter scholasticos Tunbridgienses secundo die Maii haberi solitæ coram ornatissimis ejusdem scholæ moderatoribus.

Mensis erat, mensis Maiorum nomine dictus,
Auroram Phaetontis equi jam luce vehebant,
Cum schola Tunbridgiæ, schola tantis inclyta alumnis
Pieriisque superba suis, certamina pandit.
Musa minans musæ est, et pugnat Pallade Pallas,
Græcia sidereo non sic glomeravit Olympo,
Cum facit Eliadum palmas Epeiros equarum,
Ut Mæcenatum[1] Londini ex urbe relictâ,
Tunbridgiæque scholas, atque urbis turma per arces
Pervolat huc. Rutilo postquam discumbitur ostro,
Illi aptat, primam meruit qui laude coronam,
Auro perfusam (fulgentia munera) pennam :
Et sacras alii pennas sex præmia primi
Accipiunt, meritâque caput nectuntur olivâ.
Sed quid materiam non sumo viribus æquam ?
Artes hæ (Stockwoode) tuæ, tua munera sunto.
Qualiter Æneadas terrâque marique potentes
Depinxit Maro ; seu quali lyricus ore
Pindarus Isthmiacam descripsit carmine pugnam ;
Tale tuum carmen nobis Divine poeta,
Dum mihi grammaticam pertractas ordine litem.
Hæc dici potuisse, hæc non potuisse refelli,
O schola, quam felix, quæ tot virtutibus aucta es !
Bis felix, cujus non desunt præmia laudi ;
Ter felix, præconem habeas quæ laudis Homerum."

A Latin ode mentioning the Annual Visitation.

After these verses come some of a Caleb Bridac, and, lastly, the following *tetrastichon* of Sir Robert Heath, the Chief Justice:—

" Jucunda, eximio potiaris, fronte, libello,
    Quem tibi Stockwoodi cura laborque dedit.

[1] (*Sic.*)

> Hunc cape, si cupias prædoctæ dona Minervæ,
>   Nec parvum studiis ille levamen erit."

A posthumous Grammar of his was published in 1763.

How long Stockwood was Vicar of Tonbridge is unknown: many years after his death a book written at some former time by him was published in 1763, entitled "The Treatise of the Figures at the end of the Rules of Construction in the Latin Grammar, construed. With every example applied to his Rule, for the help of the weaker sort in the Grammar Schools."

This is the last book of Stockwood's; most of them, and all his grammatical ones, were written after he had given up the School, and had become Vicar of Tonbridge.

The author explains the purpose of his little work in the following few lines:—

> "Unto the weaker sort in the Grammar School.
>   We have a proverb which doth say
>   'It is as plain as Dunstable way,'
>   The which (if ever) holdeth here,
>   Where, by construction, all so clear
>   Is made, so easy and so plain,
>   As whoso will but take the pain.
>   These figures well may understand
>   As every one doth come to hand.
>   If sluggish drones fore-slows their part,
>   Spare not, but let them feel the smart."

W. HATCH, M.A., and M. JENKINS, M.A.

1588—1640

WILLIAM HATCH was the successor of Stockwood, and Michael Jenkins succeeded Hatch; but it is most unfortunate that nothing can be found out respecting either of these Masters, excepting that Hatch was at School as a boy under Stockwood, and that he was Head Master in 1619 [1]. They were Head Masters between the years 1588 and 1640.

Nothing known of the next two Head Masters.

At the time when the Old School was pulled down, in 1863, a stone sun-dial was unearthed from beneath the scullery, bearing the date 1634 [2]. The same date is carved on the oak panelling over the fireplace in Dr. Welldon's study in his private house, together with these names of the officers of the Skinners' Company.

William Feilgate William Hewson (Wardens)	John Barnett 16 R 34 M	Thomas Covel Thomas Bayley (Wardens) 1634

From this it seems probable that some considerable internal alterations took place about this time; but whether the study was merely oak panelled or whether greater changes were made, is altogether matter for conjecture.

Probable alteration about this time in the building.

---

[1] Vide p. 89.   [2] Vide the picture of the Old School about 1790, opp. p. 60.

THOMAS HORNE, D.D.

1640—1647

DR. THOMAS HORNE was of a Nottinghamshire family, and the date of his birth was 1605. At the age of fifteen he was a student of Magdalen Hall, and in 1633 took his degree as Master of Arts. For two years he was Master of Leicester Grammar School, and after that, in 1640, he was elected to the Head Mastership of Tonbridge, where he remained for seven years. One of his sons, William Horne, was Master at Harrow; another, born at Tonbridge, was Chaplain to the Earl of St. Alban's, as well as a Fellow of King's College, Cambridge, and Senior Proctor of that University in 1682. There is an old manuscript in the School Library which contains an "inventory of the goods and books in and about the School at Tonbridge belonging to the Worshipful Company of Skinners, London, and delivered the 29th day of June, 1640, into the possession of Mr. Thomas Horne, School Master, and to be re-delivered at his departure with such others as shall

Marginalia: His education and previous position. His sons. Extract from an old MS. in the Library.

be hereafter added." The Schoolroom contained, "two long tables and two shorter tables with frames, the school wainscotted round half way, and one wainscott press for books." The inventory also mentions a workroom with a few lathes and tools in it. The other details are not interesting, and suggest that the furniture was of the most scanty description.

Dr. Horne is recorded as having "an excellent faculty in pedagogie." He wrote several educational books, of which the four following are the chief:—

1. "Janua Linguarum, or an Easy and Compendious Method and Course for the attaining all Tongues, especially the Latine, wherein are Latine sentences, 1400. By the care and study of Thom. Horne, London, 1645." These sentences, Latin on the one side of the page and English on the other, are arranged as specimens of style from the first to the fourteenth century. For instance, as an example— *His literary works,*

Of the first century:—
"Præclara accuratè agenda. Excellent things are to be done accurately." *And a specimen of them.*

Of the fourth century:—
"Improbat impugnatque viros civilis agrestes. A civil man disallows and resists clowns."

Of the seventh century:—
"Lævum pollicem fortuito luxavit. He hath put by chance his left thumb out of joint."

Of the twelfth century:—
"In ludo literario gnavus sis. Be diligent in the school."
"Ne hiulco rictu ringere. Grin not with a yawning jaw."

Of the fourteenth century:—

"Vespillo sandapilam conglutinavit. The bier-carrier sets the coffin together."

The quantity of unusual Latin words which are scattered through the book strike one as calculated to have taxed the memory of those who had to use it. However, a Latin-English Dictionary is appended to most of the editions.

2. "Manuductio in Ædem Palladis quâ utilissima methodus authores bonos legendi, indigitatur, sive de usu Authoris. Lond. 1641, 12mo." This is dedicated with a very complimentary preface to the Skinners' Company.

3. "Rhetoricæ Compendium—Latino, Anglice." London, 1651.

4. "Annotations on the Epitome of the Greek Tongue. By Ant. Laubegeois."

NICHOLAS GREY, D.D.

1647—1657

DR. NICHOLAS GREY was elected Head Master in 1647; his preferment came late in life, for he was then fifty-seven years old. His birthplace was London, and he was educated at Westminster School, and from there he went to Christ Church, Oxford, with a close studentship, at the age of sixteen. In 1614, he was appointed Head Master of the Charter House School; but as he married contrary to the statutes, he was unable to hold the office any longer. The Governors, as a mark of respect for his merits, made him Rector of Castle Camps, in Cambridgeshire. In 1624, he became Head Master of the Merchant Taylors' School; and seven years after that he was made Head Master of Eton, and a Fellow of Eton College. But when the troubles of Oliver Cromwell's time arose, Dr. Grey was ejected both from his living in Cambridgeshire and from his Fellowship at Eton. Thrown adrift, the learned but unfortunate Doctor took the office of Head Master of

His education and the vicissitudes he was subject to before he came to Tonbridge.

Tonbridge, which he held from 1647 to 1657. There is no notice of any kind about the School during this ten years, but it is satisfactory to know, that, at the Restoration, Dr. Grey was reinstated as Fellow of Eton, and obtained a parsonage there also. He died October 5, 1660, and, curiously enough, was buried at Eton, by the side of Dr. Horne, his predecessor both at Eton and Tonbridge [1].

Dr. Grey wrote the following works:—

His literary works.

1. A Dictionary in English and Latin, several times reprinted, but when first published not known.

2. "Luculenta e Sacrâ Scripturâ Testimonia ad Hugonis Grotii baptizatorum puerorum institutionem. Lond. 1647, 8vo." This is dedicated to John Hales, Fellow of Eton College.

3. "Parabolæ Evangelicæ Lat. redditæ e carmine paraphrastico varii generis, in usum Scholæ Tunbridgiensis."

[1] Wood, Athenæ Oxoniensis, vol. iii. p. 504.

JOHN GOAD, B.D.

1657—1661

THE Rev. John Goad succeeded Dr. Grey. He was by birth a Londoner, of St. Helen's Parish, Bishopsgate, and was educated at the Merchant Taylors' School. In 1632, at the age of seventeen, he obtained a Scholarship at St. John's College, Oxford, and ultimately became a Fellow of that College, taking the degree of Master of Arts in 1640. In 1643, he received the Vicarage of St. Giles, Oxford, a living attached to his College. It was in this position that the Vicar showed his parishioners a rare example of personal bravery. The King, Charles I. was at that time besieged in the town by the Parliamentary forces, and Mr. Goad persisted in performing divine service in his church, though cannon balls aimed from the adjacent camp were at the time flying all about the sacred edifice—though we are not told how large his congregation was upon this occasion. In 1646, the Chancellor of the University gave him the Vicarage of Yarnton near Oxford, and created him

His birth and education.

He held a College living at Oxford.

Bachelor of Divinity, at the age of forty-two. Eleven years after this, in 1657, he was elected Head Master of Tonbridge, where he remained till 1661. After this, he was appointed to the Mastership of the Merchant Taylors' School, an office he held for twenty years.

He became a Roman Catholic.

Mr. Goad was for many years a Roman Catholic at heart, though for some time he did not openly avow Romanism. In December, 1660, he was reconciled to the Faith of the Church of Rome, at Somerset House, by a priest belonging to the Queen Mother, Henrietta Maria, then recently returned from France; but it was not till 1686 that he declared his opinions in public. Five years previously to this declaration, the Presbyterian party, who still possessed considerable influence, suspecting him of an undue inclination[1] to Popish doctrines, in his "Comment on the Church of England Catechism," published for the use of his scholars, presented him to the Middlesex Grand Jury, and were successful in obtaining his deprivation from the Mastership of the Merchant Taylors' School. He then, under the direct patronage of the King, successfully conducted a private school in Piccadilly, till his death, in October, 1689.

He was a great meteorologist.

Mr. Goad used to draw up meteorological reports for James II., and personally presented them to the King once a month at his palace. There can be no doubt, that, for the time in which he lived, he was one of the most learned men of his day in meteorology, his works on this subject showing his acquaintance with it.

The charges of Popery which he incurred are given at length in a book called "Contrivances of the Fanatical

---

[1] Wood, Athenæ Oxon., vol. iv. p. 268, adds, "inculcated into their pates by certaine factious capricios who gaped after his place."

Conspirators in carrying on their Treasons under the umbrage of the Popish Plot laid open." In this work he is, nevertheless, described as "a most pious and learned person, so extraordinarily qualified for his profession that a better could not be found in the three kingdoms." Again, Wood, in his "Athenæ Oxonienses," vol. iv. p. 268, says, that "he had much of primitive Christianity in him, and was endowed with most admirable morals;" and, further, on his deprivation from the Mastership of the Merchant Taylors' School, that Company paid him the compliment of presenting him with a valuable gift of plate.

His death, as previously stated, took place in October, 1689, and he was buried in St. Helen's Church, near the tomb of Sir Andrew Judde.

His literary works are,—

1. A Commentary on the Catechism of the Church of England (noticed above).

2. Two Sermons preached at St. Paul's Cathedral; one entitled "The Judgment Day," delivered on the Second Sunday in Advent, 1662, and dedicated to the Masters and Wardens of the Merchant Taylors' Company, the other entitled "Prove all things." Both were published in London, 1664, in quarto.

3. "Genealogicum Latinum," for the use of Schools. London, 1676, 8vo.

4. A declaration "Whether Monarchy be the best form of Government." London, 1680, 8vo.

5. "Astro-Meteorologica[1]," or aphorisms and discourses on the Celestial Bodies, collected from observations at leisure hours during thirty years. London, 1686, folio.

[1] Lowndes' Bibliographer's Manual, vol. ii. p. 903.

6. "Auto-didactica," or a practical Vocabulary. London, 1690, in quarto.

7. "Astro-Meteorologica sana," published 1690, in quarto, after his death.

8. "Concerning Plagues, their numbers, natures and kinds." This book was burnt in the great fire of London, and was never reprinted.

9. "Diary of the weather in London, from July 1, 1677, to the last of October, 1679."

CHRISTOPHER WASE, B.D.

1661—1680

ON the retirement in 1661 of Mr. Goad, Mr. Wase, an old pupil of Dr. Grey's, was selected to fill the vacancy. Mr. Wase was educated at Eton, and in 1645 obtained a scholarship at King's College, Cambridge; he was one of the ablest men of his day, taking a great interest, suicidal indeed for his own interests, in Church and State politics. His literary talents were very considerable, and he wrote many Latin translations[1]. Of these the first was the "Electra of Sophocles, in English verse, presented to her Highness the Lady Elizabeth, with an epilogue showing the Parallel in two poems, The Return and the Restoration, 1649." This Princess Elizabeth died by poison at Carisbrook Castle at the age of fifteen, in 1650: she was the daughter of the lately-beheaded King, Charles I.

The tone of this book, and especially of its preface, got Mr. Wase into such trouble with the Parliamentarians, that

A former pupil of Dr. Grey's succeeds to the Headmastership.

[1] Lowndes' Bibliographer's Manual, vol. iii. p. 2454; vol. iv. pp. 2849, 2850.

he was deprived of his Fellowship at King's, which he then held, and was compelled to leave the country. The book itself was published at the Hague, and not in England. This is the preface: "Plagues are the mirrours wherein men's actions are reflected to their own view, which, perhaps, is the true cause that some, privy to the Ugliness of their own guilt, have issued warrants for the breaking all those looking glasses; lest their deformities should recoyl and become an eyesore to themselves. This dim Chrystall (sully'd with antiquitie and a long voyage) will returne upon your Highnesse some lines and shadows of that Pictie to your deceased Father, which seats you above the age, and beyond your years; which makes you better than your Countrey and higher than your Enemies; which lodges you in our Eye as our Example, and in our Heart as our Treasure. Be sure (most illustrious Princesse) you are not so much guarded from flattery, by the arts and vigilancy of the States, as by the Transcendencie of your own merits. The Historie of your name shall be an Academie, whence obsequious Rhetorick shall draw forth encomiums to bleach the defects of unaccomplisht Queens."

<small>His politics.</small>

On his flight from England, Mr. Wase was taken at sea, and imprisoned at Gravesend. He, however, contrived to escape, and then served in the Spanish armies against the French. He was made a prisoner in an engagement, but shortly afterwards obtained his release.

<small>He fled from England.</small>

Soon after the "Electra" appeared, a translation of Dr. Grey's edition of Hugo Grotius's Catechism from the original Latin into Greek verse was written by Mr. Wase. This was so popular, that Francis Goldsmith, of Gray's Inn, translated it into English verse; and by 1682 the book had already reached several editions.

The next contribution to the literary world was of a lighter kind. This was, in 1654, "Grotii Falisci Cynegeticon," a "Poem on Hunting, by Grotius the Faliscian, Englished and illustrated by Chr. Wase;" London, 8vo. The Poet Waller, who was then residing at Penshurst, wrote some complimentary verses to the author, which are prefixed to the book, and are worth referring to[1]. A Mr. Robert Creswell, after the preface of Waller's, adds the following lines, "To my learned and dear friend, Mr. C. Wase, upon the ensuing work:—

His poem on hunting.

Complimentary verses inscribed in it.

"If to reprieve an Author of that state
And ancestry, to rescue him from fate,
To clear him wrapt in dust, laid in the grave,
That he may here his resurrection have,
Be Pity and Justice: I approve
(My honour'd friend) your diligence of love,
Which what it likes will with great labour raise,
And of the world deserve a double praise,
As works of Charity wherein men do
Service to others, and their glory too—
Your choice commends your pains, and you did find
A Poet worthy of your equall mind,
One who may make, if this they can rehearse
Gentlemen Schollers, while they hunt in verse
One who has all the sight that man can doe,
You set him forth, and noble Waller you."

From 1661 to 1680 Mr. Wase was Master at Tonbridge, and in the first of those years he published a Latin-English

[1] Waller's Poems, p. 166.

and English-Latin Dictionary, which in 1675 was slightly remodelled and condensed into a smaller size. Charles II. granted the copyright of it for fourteen years from its first issue. It was prefaced with the very sensible remark, "This, I hope, will neither over-lighten the father's purse, nor over-load the child's satchel."

His remaining literary works.

"Cicero against Catiline," followed by the "History of France under the Ministry of Cardinal Mazarine written in Latin by Benjamin Priolo," London, both translations, were the work of the next two years. In 1678, an able tract on "Considerations on Free Schools as settled in England," printed at Oxford, drew the attention of the public. Two years after this, in 1680, Mr. Wase, for reasons unascertained, left Tonbridge.

His other works are:—

1. "Chr. Wasii Senarius, sive de Legibus et Licentiâ veterum Poetarum," Oxon. 4to, 1687. Menander, Plautus, Terence, and Aristophanes are the poets discussed.

2. "Structuræ Nonianæ" or "Lucilius bis terve castigatus."

3. Latin version of a Life of Alfred the Great, translated by John Spelman.

4. "Metra Horatiana" prefixed to Baxter's edition of Horace (1825).

He held an office in the University of Oxford.

Mr. Wase had a son who was Fellow of Corpus Christi College, Oxford, and he himself was "Superior Beadle of Civil Law," Oxon., and though of the University of Cambridge, yet was chosen Architypographus, or chief Corrector of the University Press at Oxford.

Wood, in his Athenæ Oxonienses, vol. iii. p. 884, gives a curious account of Mr. Wase's election to this office. Dr.

Fell, Dean of Christ Church, wished to force upon the electors, the Masters of Christ Church, his particular candidate. This they resented, and "a majority of the Masters, joined together (headed and encouraged chiefly by a clownish, factious person), did in despite of Dr. Fell, his mandamus and authority, of the heads of houses, seniors, and the sober party, set up and choose a mere stranger, who lived remotely from Oxon, named Christopher Wase (sometime Fellow and Bachelor of Arts of King's College in Cambridge, and afterwards a schoolmaster at several places), to the very great discomposure of Dr. Fell, and something to the discredit of the University, as if not able to afford a man to execute the said office. Afterwards Wase came to Oxon, was sworn, and took possession of his place; but Dr. Fell, who had received a character of him, would never let him execute the Archityp. place, because, as he usually said, he was not fit for it, as being not a person of sobriety, &c." *in spite of Dr. Fell's opposition.*

Mr. Wase died in 1689. During the nineteen years he was at Tonbridge, a "hall or refectory" was added, in 1676, to the back of the Head Master's house, by the Skinners' Company; and in 1663 the eastern end of the north gallery of the Parish Church was erected for the perpetual use of the School, as the arms of the Company and the inscription on it testify. *A dining-hall was built, and a gallery in the Parish Church for the use of the School.*

THOMAS HERBERT[1], eighth Earl of Pembroke, was educated under Dr. Wase; he was born 1656, and succeeded to the title in 1683, through his brother. He was Ambassador Extraordinary in 1689 to the States General, and afterwards was made a member of the Privy Council. He subsequently served in a number of different capacities; as, for *The Earl of Pembroke's career,*

---

[1] Vide p. 109.

instance, as a Colonel of Marines, and a First Commissioner of the Admiralty. He had also the offer of Lord Privy Seal, was First Plenipotentiary at the treaty of Ryswick, a Knight of the Garter, Lord High Admiral of England and Ireland, President of the Council, and seven times one of the Lords Justices at the time when his King, William III., was in Holland.

And the various appointments he held. Again, in 1702, the first year of Queen Anne's reign, he was President of the Council; in 1709 he was appointed one of the Commissioners to arrange the union between England and Scotland, and, soon afterwards, was made Lord Lieutenant of Ireland, and in 1708 Lord High Admiral of Great Britain.

At the death of Queen Anne, in 1714, George I. made him, on August 1st, a temporary Lord Justice of Great Britain, until that monarch's return from Hanover to England. *Patronage bestowed on him by Royalty.* When he took part in the coronation of the King, he was honoured with the dignity of carrying the sword called "Cortana." This King made him Lord Lieutenant of Wiltshire, Monmouth, and South Wales, as well as a member of the Privy Council. On the succession of the next Sovereign, George II., he performed the same ceremony at this coronation as at the last, and was continued in his various State offices.

His death. The Earl married three times, and his eldest son by his first wife succeeded him on his death in 1732.

THOMAS ROOTS, M.A.

1680—1714

ON the retirement of Mr. Wase, the Rev. Thomas Roots, of St. John's College, Oxford, was nominated as Head Master. He took his degree of M.A. in 1666, and had the care of the School from 1680 to 1714. Nothing is known of him personally, but his son was educated at the School under Dr. Wase together with Thomas Herbert, Earl of Pembroke. This son, Mr. Richard Roots, wrote "Short Instructions for the Sacrament," printed at Oxford; to which is prefixed a dedication to his patron, Thomas, Earl of Pembroke and Montgomery, which is so honourable to two Tonbridge scholars that a part of it is worth inserting here. "My Lord," says he, " it is a great satisfaction to a heart full of gratitude to ease itself by a thankful confession. And as this is all the return I have hitherto had an opportunity of making for the many repeated favours I have received from your Lordship, from my first going to the University to your placing me in

Little is known of this Head Master.

His son Richard.

The dedication of his book to his patron.

the station I now am in; so I thought it my duty to make my first public appearance with a public acknowledgement. And I hope your Lordship will lay aside the severity of your judgement, while you read over this little treatise, which has nothing but plainness and shortness to recommend it; besides its carrying the title of Religion in its frontispiece, which always finds an easy admission to your Lordship, whose just character is great and good, faithful to Cæsar and faithful to God.

"May God and Cæsar always have such servants to adorn, as well as support, both the Church and Crown, to both which your Lordship has been eminently serviceable, and I can, without being contradicted by envy, say you have feared God and honoured the Queen: For, in discharge of your duty to God, your own exemplary piety shines forth with extraordinary brightness; and the good order of your whole family deserves the character of having a Church in your house. And in discharge of your duty to Her Majesty, your unspotted reputation defies detraction, and the rankest malice must own, that, as your Lordship has passed through all the highest offices, so have you shewn yourself equal to all, have discharged all with capacity, fidelity, and honour; and have represented your Sovereign, both by sea and land, with such glory and success, that the whole nation justly prays for your Lordship next to her most excellent Majesty herself, and the established succession of the House of Hanover; and doubts not that posterity will be as happy in your most hopeful and numerous progeny, as the present age is in your Lordship, to whom more kingdoms than one own themselves obliged; and I hope your Lordship will allow me to join in the general acclamation, and will forgive the innocent pride I take in declaring to the world, that I call him Patron whom the public call Benefactor, which is an honour too great either to be deserved or concealed, by your Lordship's most obliged, most grateful, and most humble servant, RICHARD ROOTS."

This Earl of Pembroke presented to him the valuable rectories of Chilmark and Bishopstone in Wiltshire; and he also gave to his brother William (a Fellow of Magdalen College, Oxford) the living of Hatfield in Hertfordshire.

In 1693, a dispute arose about the freedom of the School, which was settled by Lord Chancellor Yorke to belong to boys residing " in villâ et patriâ adjacente."

Dispute about the freedom of the School.

RICHARD SPENCER, M.A

1714—1743

FROM 1714 to 1743, the Rev. Richard Spencer was Head Master. He is supposed to have written several works, but the only two extant are an edition of a book called " Bellum Grammaticale," 1625, in the style of Plautus and Terence, together with a work edited anonymously by him, called " Introductiones duæ ad poetas intelligendas, &c., in usum Scholæ Tunbridgiensis, 1729." The former book is a great curiosity, and in its day was very noted. This is its title,—" Bellum Grammaticale, sive Nominum Verborumque Discordia Civilis : Tragico-Comœdia ab eruditissimis Oxoniensibus adinventa, et summo cum applausu in scenam producta, olim apud Oxonienses coram serenissimâ Elizabethâ Anglorum reginâ, iterum, in scholâ Pellionum apud Tunbridgienses, 1718, in omnium illorum, qui ad Grammaticam animos appellunt, oblectamentum edita. Excudebat, Joh. Spencerus, Collegii Sionis Londiniensis Bibliothecarius, 1635. Editio hæc altera et

The "Bellum Grammaticale."

Its Latin title,

multo emendatior, curâ Richardi Spenceri, Scholæ Tunbridgiensis Magistri, Lond. 1726."

The prologue of sixteen lines is so illustrative of the style of the book, that it would be a pity to omit it.

And prologue.

" Hoc agite, si vultis (spectatores benevoli),
   Quos solos adesse speramus et cupimus. Tragico-comœdiam
Vobis dabimus, nobis si ames et oculis dare est otium :
Non quæ lacrymas exprimas, sed risum moveat ;
Nam belli funesti et luctuosi sim licet nuncius
Quo florentissimam Grammaticæ provinciam miserè
Vexarunt Poeta et Amo, seditiosi Principes :
Non sine lamentabili strage fortissimorum Verborum et
   Nominum ;
Plus tamen delectationis faciet et lætitiæ,
Quam doloris et luctus, quòd, spectatores, non auctores eritis
In tam tristi certamine : quod si vobis ridiculi
Videbimur, quod rem in Scenam producimus ridiculam,
Decorum nos observare existimabitis, ut in fabulis decet
Materiam qui sumpsimus nostris convenientem viribus
Date operam, adesto æquo animo, per silentium,
Ut pernoscatis belli tam atrocis principium et exitum.

The prologue to the " Bellum Grammaticale."

DRAMATIS PERSONÆ.

In Castris Nominum.

Porta, **Rex** Nominum.
Ego, **Dux** Pronominum.
Papæ, **Dux** Interjectionum.
Cis, **Regina** Præpositionum.
Ille, Parasitus Poetæ.
Adjectivum in **Neutro** Genere.

The Dramatis Personæ.

I

In Castris Verborum.

The Dramatis Personæ.

Amo, Rex Verborum.
Ædepol, Dux Adverbiorum.
Sodes, Legatus.

Ubique, Parasitus
Edo, Verbum.
Sum, Fugitivus.

Participium, Dux Insidiatus.
Fors, Nuncia.
Simul, Dux Conjunctionum.

Quamvis, } Præcones.
Tamen,   }

Solœcismus,
Barbarismus,   } Grammaticæ Pestes.
Traulismus,
Cacatonus

Priscianus,
Linacrus,   } Grammaticæ Judices.
Despauterius,
Lilius,

Scena—Grammaticæ Provincia."

A copy of this work is extant.

Such is the plan of one of these old Tonbridge plays, which were annually performed on "Skinners' Day" for two centuries and a half. Of this work in particular there is a copy in the British Museum; of similar plays a specimen will be found at the end of the book. The boys who acted in the plays had each to pay a small fine, or were in later times expected to make a donation towards the School library, which was built during Mr. Cawthorn's time. An entry in one of the library MS. books says:—

"Benefactors to the library from the year 1718 to 1725.
"The scholars that then acted the Bellum Grammaticale gave 1*l*. 15*s*."

<small>Extract from a MS. in the School library concerning the old Tonbridge plays.</small>

The first known gratuity that was given to the Master in addition to his salary, was in 1721, when on June 8th, it was ordered by the Skinners' Company, that "twenty guineas be given to Richard Spenser, schoolmaster of Tunbridge School, to encourage his care and diligence therein," and, June 13th, 1734, "five guineas to Mr. Elcock, usher, for the year last past." Again, in 1742, June 17th, "thirty guineas to Richard Spenser, and ten guineas to Mr. John Maynott, usher." These sums continued to be paid annually for many years.

JAMES CAWTHORN, M.A.

1743—1761

Rev. J. Cawthorn's early education.

UPON the resignation of Mr. Spencer, the Rev. James Cawthorn filled his place. He is known to the public as a poet, beginning, about the age of seventeen, in 1738, the same year that he went to Clare Hall, Cambridge, with "The Perjured Lover." He was born at Sheffield, and was educated partly in a school at Kirby Lonsdale, Westmoreland, and partly at Rotherham, Yorkshire. While at the former school he started a periodical called "The Tea Table," probably more laudable for its aim, than for actual literary merits. After leaving the University, he was Usher to Martin Clare[1], author of the "Treatise on Fluids," whose daughter he married; but their children

[1] There is an inscription in the first volume of the Philosophical Transactions, in the School Library at Tonbridge, in the following words:—"Bibliothecæ Scholæ publicæ grammaticalis apud Tunbrigienses, comitatu Cantii; in usum studiosæ juventutis, humanioribus literis ibidem incumbentis, sub auspiciis generi sui doctissimi Jacobi Cawthorn, ejusdem Scholæ Archididasculi—Martinus Clare, A.M. F.R.S. Dono dedit. Anno 1745."

died in infancy. Indeed, his most beautiful poem is "A Father's Extempore Consolation," written on the death of his twin children. In 1743 he went to Tonbridge, and gained a reputation for great strictness and severity. His character was peculiar; though harsh in school matters, in society he was pleasant; with a great love of fine arts, he was passionately fond of music, and yet this was almost the only art with which he had no technical acquaintance. He was a bad horseman, but a constant rider; indeed, he had been known to ride from Tonbridge to London, to hear a concert, between the afternoon of one day and seven o'clock in the morning of the next. He was constantly in the habit of giving his boys lessons in rhetoric every week, throwing on the floor of the School-room a Virgil or Shakespeare, or some such book, and challenging any of his pupils to speak a speech against him. It is a notable example of the system of oral and colloquial instruction, now too much shelved to make room for book learning, which was much in vogue at that time. *His character and fondness for literature and music. His system of oral instruction.*

Mr. Cawthorn's works were published by subscription in 1771. Among the list of subscribers are many of the surrounding gentry, as J. Children, Esq., W. Scoones, Esq., William Woodgate, Esq., of Summer Hill, Sir Sampson Gideon, Rev. Johnson Towers, Master of Tonbridge School, several of the Woodfalls, and the Master of the Skinners' Company, to whom the book is dedicated. The editor, by mistake, attributes to him, and inserts in his collection, a little poem called "Poverty and Poetry," of which he was not the author. His imitation of Pope's "Abelard to Eloisa," however peculiar the subject, shows much depth of feeling; and his collection of poems proves him capable *His literary works.*

of great variety of power, from the gay style of Horace, to solid reflection and satires on men and manners. He composed several dialogues for the annual recitations on "Skinners' Day." In the year of his death he had appointed Virgil's fifth Eclogue for the approaching visitation. Eight of these dialogues are given in "Chalmers' English Poets," vol. xiv. p. 229. These are the subjects:—

His dialogues for "Skinners' Day."

(1) 1746. "The equality of human conditions."
(2) 1752. "Nobility: a moral essay."
(3) 1753. "Lady Jane Grey to Lord Guildford Dudley: an epistle. In the manner of Ovid."
(4) 1755. "The regulation of the passions the source of human happiness: a moral essay."
(5) 1756. "Of Taste: an essay."
(6) 1757. "Wit and Learning: an allegory."
(7) 1760. "Life Unhappy, because we use it improperly: a moral essay."
(8) 1760. "The Temple of Hymen: a tale."

He printed two occasional sermons in 1746, one of which was preached before the Governors of the School at St. Antholin's, in London. Lord Eardley was at School under Mr. Cawthorn, and though he never mentioned his Master's name without trepidation, yet as a mark of respect he bought for him the next presentation to a valuable living, which, however, did not become vacant during his life. That life was unfortunately cut short by an accident which happened in 1761. Mr. Cawthorn was out for a ride, and while his horse was preparing to drink at the pond opposite the house built by Mr. Hayton, and since bought by Mr. Deacon, on Quarry Hill, Tonbridge, it stumbled and threw its rider. This caused Mr. Cawthorn an injury of a broken

His accidental death.

leg, which, in a few days after, April 15, proved fatal to him. A tradition since that time has been handed down in the School that the ghost of the stern master perambulated the dormitories of the old building at midnight on April 15, with clanking chains and measured step. Hence any boy will tell you who Mr. Cawthorn was, while all the other Head Masters are almost a dead letter to them. The tradition in the School about him.

The Skinners' Company in 1760 united with the Head Master in building a library at the south end of the School; it is just apparent on the left-hand side in the print opposite page 60. He aided in building a library.

Mr. Cawthorn was buried in the Church of Tonbridge, under the School Gallery. A neat mural monument of marble contains the following inscription:—" Hic sepultus, jacet Jacobus Cawthorn, A.M., Scholæ Tunbrigiensis Magister, qui juventuti tam literis quam moribus instituendæ, operam, magno non sine honore, dedit. Integer—comes— et omnibus carus, vixit. Valde desideratus—heu citius! obiit Ap. 15$^{mo.}$ 1761. Ætat. suæ 49. Opibus quas multis largâ manu distribuit, fruetur, et in æternum fruetur. Soror mœsta ex grato animo hoc posuit." His monument in the Church.

WILLIAM WOODFALL was at school about 1745. He is well known by the name of " Memory " Woodfall, as having possessed that most marvellous faculty of memory and fluency which served him so well during his life, and preserved his name to posterity as a man of literary talent. While at school his ability was put to the test, and so successfully underwent the ordeal, that it would be an injustice to omit the only mention of his youth that is generally known or acknowledged. His master, Mr. Cawthorn, set him one evening a book of Homer to learn by heart, an imposition " Memory " Woodfall's ability.

characteristic of the times in general, and of the master who set it in particular. The next morning Woodfall repeated it word for word to Mr. Cawthorn, who, capable of appreciating such rare talent, was so affected as to burst into tears. To follow Woodfall here through his life would be too heavy a task; a few words will give a sufficient outline.

Woodfall was editor and reporter of the "Morning Chronicle" about 1769, and afterwards attached himself to a paper called the "Diary." His great work was, however, the editorship of the "Public Advertiser," in which Junius' Letters appeared. His practice was to secure, by arriving long before the time, a good seat in the House of Commons, and then, with merely a hard-boiled egg for sustenance, he frequently sat for eight or a dozen hours eagerly listening to the animated and frequently stormy debates. Reporting parliamentary debates when no written notes were allowed to be taken, and when one reporter for each newspaper was the maximum allowance of the Houses of Parliament, was a very arduous task. With not a single note, and his memory as his only aid, he used, after remaining in the house thus for hours together, to go home and write such accurate, animated, and life-like reports, that he quickly raised the reputation of his paper as well as his own in public estimation. Reporters in his time were frequently apt to be several days behindhand with their reports, which consequently were often feeble and inaccurate. But punctuality was Woodfall's watchword, and intense application one of his characteristics. However, there sprung up a system of reporters taking turns by the hour or so to report the debates, and this in the end overwhelmed Woodfall. Long did he bravely carry on single-handed the unequal contest,

He edited Junius' Letters.

His great aptitude for reporting.

but at last Woodfall's newspaper waned. The "London Society," in an article in one of its numbers in 1864, describes him as "a rather taciturn man, holding no communication with those around him, wholly absorbed in the business, retaining his seat from the beginning to the end of the proceedings, and only satisfying the demands of appetite with the hard-boiled egg which he brought from home in his pocket, and which it was the special delight of the young wags, his rivals, slyly to abstract from its depository and substitute an unboiled one in its stead, an annoyance for which Woodfall never failed to certify his resentment by every demonstration which so silent and self-contained a man could make[1]." There is also an engraving of Woodfall in this number of "London Society," taken from a portrait in the possession of the family, with "'Memory' Woodfall, the father of modern reporting," printed underneath.

Quotation from the "London Society."

---

[1] I have an autograph letter of Woodfall's, inviting an ancestor of mine to dinner, to meet several literary men of the day.—S. R.

JOHNSON TOWERS, M.A.

1761—1770

<small>Mr. Tower's education and literary work.</small>

UPON the death of Mr. Cawthorn, the Rev. Johnson Towers became Master of the School. He was born in 1729 at Kendal, in Westmoreland, and afterwards went to Queen's College, Oxford. At the time of his appointment to Tonbridge, 1761, he was Master of the Grammar School at Wye, Kent. Previously to that he had been Rector of Pett, Sussex, and while there he edited a text of Cæsar's Commentaries, and wrote a translation to it. There is a second edition of this book in the School Library, dated 1768. Dr. Thomas Knox speaks very highly of Mr. Towers and his book, affirming that, had not translations in general been looked upon then with such an unfavourable eye by School Masters, this Cæsar would have

<small>Second dispute about the freedom of the School.</small>

been still better received than it was. In 1764 another warm dispute arose as to the limits of the freedom of the School, and the matter was referred to the Lord Chancellor, Mr. Yorke, Sir F. Norton, De Grey, Blackstone, and Hussey. Their decision was that "children of the town and parish of Tunbridge who could write competently and read Latin and English perfectly should be instructed on proper application to the Master, without payment of any consideration, excepting the statutable entrance fee." But Judge Blackstone was of opinion that the College of "All Saints" ought to have been consulted.

Mr. Towers gave up his connexion with the School in 1770, and three years afterwards died, and was buried at Sandon, in Essex.

LORD WHITWORTH [1] was educated partly under Mr. Cawthorn and partly under Mr. Towers. Among his Schoolfellows were Lord Eardley, Colonel James, of Tytham Lodge, Kent, and a Christopher Hull, of Sidcup, to whom he was "fag." Every body is aware that it was this celebrated nobleman who, during the peace of Amiens, was twice publicly insulted by Napoleon, when in the performance of his duty as English ambassador at Paris. Before this, Lord Whitworth had been an officer in the Guards; he had also filled official posts at the courts of Russia, Poland, and Copenhagen, and had been a Privy Councillor. He then retired to Knowle, his country-seat, where he raised, at his own expense, the Holmesdale battalion of infantry, six hundred strong. In 1813 he was made a peer of England (previously having been an Irish peer, with the Order of the Bath), and Viceroy of Ireland. This post he resigned in 1817, and soon after died. He was a benevolent man in private life, and in public was always considered an example of an accomplished English gentleman. One of his last acts was to spend a thousand pounds in employing old people on farm-work about his residence at Knowle.

[1] Gentleman's Magazine, 1825.

VICESIMUS KNOX, LL.B.

1771—1778

His education in London, and at Oxford.

He resided in London for a time.

THE Rev. Vicesimus Knox followed Mr. Towers as Head Master in 1771. His father was a London merchant, and he himself was educated in London, at the Merchant Taylors' School. He then went to St. John's College, Oxford, and took a fellowship there connected with his School. From Oxford he returned to the Merchant Taylors' School as Second Master, and whilst in London for some time aided Dr. John Jortin as morning preacher at St. Dunstan's in the East. He was only seven years at Tonbridge, as he was compelled to retire in 1778 from ill-health, and in 1780 he died at Penshurst, where, on his resigning his post at the School, he had taken up his residence. During these years there was an average of about eight boarders in the school-house, but the numbers of the whole School then are not known.

ANTHONY HART[1] was born in the West Indies about

---

[1] Foss's Lives of the Judges, from which this is taken *literatim*.

1754, and was at Tonbridge under the first Dr. Vicesimus Knox. His education in England was with a view to being called to the bar, and in 1781 he became an Equity barrister. For forty-six years he incessantly worked, gaining a great acquaintance with law and a large practice. His characteristic was a remarkable clearness in his statements, together with an unostentatious fluency that won for him general admiration and respect. In 1827 he was appointed Vice-Chancellor of England and in the next year he succeeded Lord Manners as Lord Chancellor of Ireland. A joke of Lord Norbury's on the occasion is told by Foss in his Lives of the Judges of England, " that the Government had treated the Irish with their wonted injustice;— deprived them of what they needed, and given them what they already possessed,—taken away *Manners*, and gave them *Heart*." The esteem shown for him on his removal in 1830 was manifested in an affecting scene at his departure. His death happened in December, 1831.

Sir Anthony Hart's career.

VICESIMUS KNOX, D.D.

1778—1812

His birth

VICESIMUS KNOX, D.D.[1], was born on the 8th of December, 1752, and was the only son of the Rev. Vicesimus Knox, LL.B., a Fellow of St. John's College, Oxford; afterwards a Master of Merchant Taylors' School; and lastly, Head Master of Tonbridge School. His father

And education.

educated him privately at home until the age of fourteen, when, in consequence of his urgent entreaties to be placed at a public school, he entered Merchant Taylors' in a high class, under the Rev. James Townley. This gentleman possessed great urbanity, which recommended him to the friendship of Garrick. Although not a profound scholar, yet he was distinguished by a refined literary taste, which he was remarkably successful in imparting among his pupils.

---

[1] This life is taken, nearly word for word, from a biographical preface, written by his son Dr. Thomas Knox, to the Works of Vicesimus Knox, D.D., 7 vols. 8vo, 1824. Vide also Biographical Dictionary of Living Authors, 1816. Public Characters of 1803-4, London, 1804. Rose's Biographical Dictionary, 1857. Cate's Dictionary of General Biography, 1867.

VICESIMUS KNOX, D.D

Dr. Knox spoke of him with gratitude, attributing, in no small degree, his own studious habits, while others of his age were wholly addicted to trifling amusements, to the flattering but judicious encouragement he received from his Master. His exercises were publicly read in the School, as models of excellence.

It will be seen in his " Liberal Education " that he gives the preference decisively to a public education. In his own particular instance he was capable of forming most accurately the comparison. Notwithstanding the peculiar advantages he enjoyed in a course of private education from the zealous labours of an affectionate parent, who was highly qualified for the office of a tutor, the stimulus of emulation was still wanting, and he declared that, in a very short time, he made a much greater proficiency at school. At this susceptible period of life, he had the happiness and good fortune of enjoying an intimacy with that most amiable divine and classical scholar, Dr. Jortin, and with that eminent genius, Oliver Goldsmith; the former frequently invited him to pass his holidays at his vicarage at Kensington, and, together with the latter (whom he also often visited, and who took a great interest in his studies), contributed to confirm that ardent love of literature in his youthful mind that never afterwards forsook him. *His early preference for a public school.*

At the age of nearly nineteen, he was elected to a Fellowship at St. John's College[1], where his father had preceded him; and a riper and a sounder scholar, perhaps, never entered within its walls. In consequence of the reputation that he immediately acquired at Oxford, especially from his Latin verses, he was selected for one of the speakers at the *His election to a Fellowship.*

[1] His name is entered in the College books as " Knock, B.C.L., Oct. 19, 1753."

Encænia, when Lord North was installed Chancellor. He remained eight years at the university, a longer residence than is now usual; but after taking his Bachelor's degree he had devoted himself to general literature, and he there found in the numerous libraries to which he procured access an inexhaustible source of mental gratification, which he was unwilling to relinquish. At this time he assiduously cultivated the practice of English composition, and before he finally left Oxford sent anonymously, as a present to Mr. Dilly (the Bookseller), the manuscript of a sufficient number of the "Essays, Moral and Literary," to make a volume, leaving it at his option to publish or destroy them, as he might be advised. Dr. Johnson was consulted, who spoke of the style and matter in terms of the highest panegyric, and predicted the future fame of the writer. The work appeared at first in one volume; numerous impressions were speedily required, and it was soon extended to three volumes. The author was no longer concealed. His name at once burst into eminence, and the public voice placed him in the first rank of the English Classics. In no department of the Belles Lettres has any publication, excepting the "Spectator," been so extensively circulated. It has been translated into most of the European languages.

<small>His first literary work.</small>

Upon the resignation of his father in 1778, Dr. Knox was appointed to the Head Mastership of Tonbridge School. He adopted this profession in opposition to the remonstrances of Dr. Dennis, the President of St. John's, and Dr. Wheeler, the learned public orator; both of whom feared, without reason, as it proved in the result, that so laborious an undertaking would injuriously interfere with the literary career he had so successfully commenced. Mrs. Montague

<small>His appointment to Tonbridge.</small>

also, who then enjoyed high celebrity, and several other eminent characters of that day, took considerable pains to persuade him to dedicate himself to the academic life at Oxford, which they represented as offering to him the most brilliant prospects; but an attachment to an accomplished and excellent lady, the daughter of Thomas Miller, Esq., of Tonbridge, whom he subsequently married, unalterably fixed his determination.

The duties of the office in which he was engaged necessarily directed his attention to the best modes of forming the classical scholar, and in 1781 he published his treatise entitled "Liberal Education." The success of this work was not less than that of the "Essays," it having long superseded all others upon this important subject. In pointing out the defects in education, he could not pass over the gross relaxation of discipline in the Universities which at that time prevailed, more especially at Oxford; nor could he, consistently with his purpose, refrain from exposing certain absurdities, that rendered the public exercises ridiculous, and defeated their objects. Whatever resentment was felt in the universities at the moment, the suggestions of the author have since been regarded; a reform has taken place in many of the objectionable particulars; and he lived to express great satisfaction at the admirable spirit of emulation among the students, which the recent statutable regulations have produced. Had his life been spared, he had intended, in a new edition, to have expunged many of those strictures, which, happily, he considered no longer applicable.

His views on liberal education.

In 1787 he published a series of miscellaneous papers, under the title of "Winter Evenings." A biographer in the "British Essayists" thus speaks of them: "The work entitled 'Winter Evenings' contains a great variety of amusement and instruction. The literary essays will generally be found to evince a mind well stored with learning, and with learning not lying in a state of lumber, but judiciously arranged and tastefully combined. Dr. Knox had a nice perception of the beautiful, and, like the best of the Greeks, he united the beautiful with the good. His moral feelings were in strict union with a cultivated taste. His 'Winter Evenings,' in almost every page, furnish ample proofs of a mind that was perpetually labouring to promote a proficiency both in literature and virtue, and to diffuse a pure and hallowed regard both for the beautiful and the good."

About this time he had the honour of receiving from Philadelphia a diploma, conferring a Doctor's degree in that university[1], with a unanimous expression of the high sense that learned body entertained of the services that his works, which had all been republished in America, had rendered to the cause of learning and morals. For the use of his own School, which had risen to great reputation (although it had not acquired during his Mastership the advantage of the very opulent endowment which, by a decree of the Court of Chancery, it now possesses), he edited Horace and Juvenal upon the *expurgata* plan; and originated and superintended those well-known and useful compilations, "Elegant Extracts[2]," in prose and verse; "Elegant Epistles," "Family Lectures," &c., the prefaces to which were written by himself.

---

[1] Offered him, it is said, at the request of Charles Dilly, the bookseller.

[2] Among these is a poem called "The Tonbridge School-boy," spoken by his son, Thomas Knox, at the Annual Visitation on May 9, 1802.

In 1793 appeared "Personal Nobility," in one volume, "containing advice to a young nobleman, in a series of letters, on the conduct of his studies, and the best means of maintaining the dignity of the peerage." The abolition of nobility in France had taken place at this period, and given a particular interest to the subject of this work, which is written in a glowing strain of eloquence, and is not less replete with judicious precepts than constitutional opinions. It was in this year that he preached his celebrated sermon at Brighton. He had long been deeply impressed with the folly and wickedness of war. The subject of this sermon was the "*Unlawfulness of offensive War.*" Some subaltern militia officers, hoping to recommend themselves to notice, under the pretence of reprobating the doctrines inculcated in this discourse, disgraced themselves by making a riot at the theatre to which, a few evenings afterwards, he had accompanied his family, and compelling him, together with his wife and young children, to quit it. Dr. Knox treated this unmanly aggression with contempt, and abstained from any legal proceedings, contenting himself with publishing in his own vindication the strongest passages of the sermon, the whole of which is here printed. He shortly afterwards followed up this subject by giving a translation of the tract of Erasmus, entitled, "*Bellum dulce inexpertis.*" This translation he called "Antipolemus."

At the beginning of 1795 he wrote "The Spirit of Despotism." He composed this treatise under a conviction that the continental confederacy to crush the rising liberties of France was directed against the best interests of mankind; and that it received its principal support from England. This he attributed to the influence of that pernicious spirit that he has described under the appellation of the Spirit of Despotism, and which he thought was encouraged by the writings of Mr. Burke. Shortly after the work was finished, the war assumed altogether a new character, and the French in their turn became the aggressors, in the name of Liberty seeking military glory, destroying the independence of neighbouring nations, and undermining all the foundations of freedom. He determined, therefore, to postpone the publication until a more favourable opportunity, which, from the course of political events, did not occur during his life. Indeed, during his latter years, theology became his principal concern. It happened, however, that a copy of this work escaped the custody to which it was confided, and, without his knowledge, was published. The writer already quoted thus expresses himself upon the subject of it. "No one can doubt but that the love of liberty in the bosom of Dr. Knox was not merely a transient feeling but a permanent principle, for he cherished it at the expense of great worldly interests. The work entitled 'The Spirit of Despotism,' which was not till lately generally known to be his production, evinces a higher tone of thought, more fire of sentiment, and more force of expression, than will readily be found in his other works. Indeed, a calmer style was more suited to Essays on literary or miscellaneous topics. No work is better calculated than 'The Spirit of Despotism,' to unfold the deformities and to excite a detestation of arbitrary power."

His Spirit of Despotism.

The "Sermons upon Faith, Hope, and Charity," in one volume 8vo, were published about this period, and were followed by "Christian Philosophy," in two volumes, which was intended by the author chiefly as an antidote to the doctrines of those who call themselves, by way of eminence,

His volume of sermons.

"*Rational Christians*," and who, neglecting the peculiar doctrines of Christianity, insinuated that moral duties constituted the whole of it. Shortly afterwards appeared "Considerations on the Nature and Efficacy of the Lord's Supper;" the principal object of which was to assert the important truth, "that benefits are annexed to the reception of the Eucharist," in opposition to Bishops Hoadley and Pearce, Drs. Sykes, Balguy, and Bell. That eminent theologian, Bishop Horsley, with a liberality that did him honour, as his politics were known to be at variance with the author's, publicly eulogized this treatise in the charges delivered to his clergy, recommending it to their particular perusal; and he made it the occasion of soliciting the friendship of the writer, which continued till the Bishop's death. *And work on the Lord's Supper.*

The reputation which Dr. Knox had acquired in the Belles Lettres was fully sustained by his works in theology. They display an elevated tone of piety, his usual polished style, and most learnedly enforce doctrines of the soundest divinity. It was his singular fate to give offence to those sects in religion which differ widely from each other, the Unitarians and the Methodists. Dr. Disney (of the Essex-street Chapel) published a series of letters addressed to him upon his opinions expressed in his sermons; and the Methodists, although he vindicated some of their tenets from misrepresentation, sorely felt his animadversions upon the mischiefs occasioned by their extravagance and fanaticism. *His disagreement from sects of opposite character.*

Dr. Knox left Tonbridge in 1812, and retired to London, where he purchased the beautiful residence of Owen Williams, Esq., M.P., upon the Adelphi Terrace. In the year of his departure from the School, he received a gift " from several scholars, who chose to be anonymous, to be laid out under his direction for the library[1]." He was Rector of Runwell and Ramsden Crays in Essex (of which parishes he was the patron), and minister of the parochial chapelry of Shipbourn in Kent, where he performed the duty, for nearly forty years, with exemplary regularity. After his retirement, while he lived in London, the situation of his benefices not permitting him to live on them, he never withheld his powerful aid from the pulpit, whenever it was solicited in favour of the various charities with which the metropolis abounds. There are few of those institutions which have not benefited by his exertions. During this period he preached at Bedford Chapel, Bloomsbury, the very eloquent and persuasive sermon that is included in the sixth volume of his works "upon the duty and advantage of educating the poor." A few other single sermons that he printed are contained in that volume. In one of them, which he preached at the opening of the chapel of the Philanthropic Society, in St. George's Fields, he first called the public attention to the necessity of increasing the number of the places of worship on the establishment. As a preacher, he will long be remembered: his voice was powerful and melodious; his matter was always excellent; and his manner possessed a dignity, propriety, and impressiveness that riveted the attention of the most crowded congregations.

In the last year of his life he published a pamphlet against the "Degradation of Grammar Schools." A bill was then pending in Parliament for the general education of the poor; among its provisions was one which would have had the effect of lowering the education now afforded in the ancient Grammar Schools, by giving instruction in writing, reading, and arithmetic under the same roof, as a co-ordinate part

---

[1] Extract from a MS. in the School library.

of the foundation, to an humbler class of scholars out of the funds exclusively appropriated by the donors to the learned languages. The bill was withdrawn. It afforded, however, a subject for a splendid defence of classical education. The arguments of Milton, Locke, Bacon, and others, who recommend the teaching boys *things*, in preference to the classics, are successfully combated.

His politics were founded on philanthropy. To preserve peace and secure liberty he deemed the first object of government, considering that all other public benefits necessarily follow in their train. He thought the whig doctrines, as asserted at the revolution, consulted the happiness of the human race in preference to the particular interests of certain privileged classes and individuals. He was a whig, therefore, upon principle. His steadiness and consistency were remarkable. Holding time-serving in abhorrence, he scorned any concealment of his political opinions, however disadvantageous to his own private interests might be the avowal. It will hereafter excite surprise, that one to whom the public owed such important obligations should have derived no benefit from the public patronage; but the ascendency of the Tory party during his life, excepting a few brief intervals, will account for his exclusion from ministerial favour. In one of those intervals, shortly after the formation of the ministry of Mr. Fox, in 1806, he received an intimation from him, that he was designed for promotion to one of the highest stations in the Church. Unhappily, for the best interests of the establishment, this intention was frustrated by the death of that enlightened statesman (followed shortly by the dissolution of the administration), before the opportunity occurred of carrying it into effect.

His character and opinions.

His views on religious toleration.

This circumstance, on his own account, occasioned in his breast no regrets; for preferment was never his object, nor occupied his thoughts. He was, from conscientious conviction, a firm friend of the Church of England, but, at the same time, an advocate of a liberal toleration. Entertaining much respect for the private character of Bishop Dampier, he felt it his duty to protest against an address which that Bishop produced, with more zeal than discretion, at the *altar*, for the signature of the clergy assembled at a visitation of his diocese, thanking the Crown for requiring a pledge from the administration, that they would never again agitate the Catholic question. He was aware that differences of opinion might conscientiously be entertained upon this subject, but thought, with the excellent Bishop Bathurst, that, with proper securities, it was no less contrary to sound policy and justice than to the benign spirit of the Gospel, to impose civil disabilities upon so many of the Christian subjects of the United Kingdom, merely because they remained faithful to the religion of their forefathers.

His scholarship.

Dr. Knox possessed extraordinary facility in composition of every kind. He wrote and spoke Latin with the most classical purity. He was singularly felicitous in epigrammatic point, and a very eminent Greek scholar. He was a great student of the harmony of language, invariably forming his sentences with a regard to rhythmical proportion.

The amiable sentiments which abound in all his works portray with fidelity the qualities that adorned his private character. He possessed the acutest sensibility, and his heart was exquisitely susceptible of all the charities of domestic life. His habits were unobtrusive and retired, and his whole demeanour in society was marked by a diffidence inseparable from his nature.

It has been remarked that he did not display the extraordinary fertility of mind in conversation which distinguishes his writings. This observation might reasonably be made by one who knew him only in the latter years of his life; not that there was any decay of his faculties, as is evident from his powerful pamphlet on Classical Learning, written a few months only before his death; but, from a succession of domestic calamities, he suffered greatly from mental depression, which, unfortunately, attacked him with particular violence in company, and was the cause of his silence. At no distant intervals he had to deplore the loss of a son in the flower of his age, of his own wife, and of an only daughter, the wife of R. C. Sconce, Esq. Before these grievous afflictions his conversation was distinguished as much by the riches of his well-stored mind as by the native vigour of his intellect, set off by a delightful fervour of expression, and often relieved by a most agreeable playfulness. His conversational powers.

Dr. Knox enjoyed remarkably good health, the consequence of an excellent constitution, as well as of regular habits. He was always an early riser. His reading was almost universal, comprehending all the best authors in the living as well as dead languages. He was enabled to follow his literary pursuits with unabated ardour till within the last three days of his life. The strength of his constitution seemed to promise an extreme old age, when he was seized with an inflammation of the intestines, while on a visit at his son's house at Tonbridge, which terminated his life on the 6th of September, 1821, in the sixty-ninth year of his age. So little foreseen was this melancholy event, that he was under an engagement to preach a sermon at Limehouse, a few days after it happened, for the benefit of the National Schools. His death.

And funeral.

His funeral took place at Tonbridge, on which occasion the inhabitants of that town and neighbourhood spontaneously assembled in a very numerous body, to offer a reverential tribute of regret.

A monument has been erected in the chancel of Tonbridge Church with this inscription :—

The inscription on his tablet in Tonbridge Church.

TO THE MEMORY OF
VICESIMUS KNOX, D.D.
MASTER OF TONBRIDGE SCHOOL, AND RECTOR OF RUNWELL AND RAMSDEN CRAYS IN ESSEX.
BORN DEC. 8, 1752.—DIED SEPT. 6, 1821.

A SOUND DIVINE,
AN ELEGANT AND PROFOUND SCHOLAR,
A POLISHED AND POWERFUL WRITER,
AN ELOQUENT, ZEALOUS, AND PERSUASIVE PREACHER OF THE GOSPEL,
HE EMPLOYED HIS HIGH ENDOWMENTS
TO THE GLORY OF GOD
AND THE MORAL AND INTELLECTUAL IMPROVEMENT OF MAN.
ANXIOUS EVER TO ADVANCE THE HAPPINESS OF HIS FELLOW-CREATURES,
UPON THE PUREST PRINCIPLES OF CHRISTIAN PHILANTHROPY,
WITH A LOFTY SPIRIT OF INDEPENDENCE,
AND A RARE DISINTERESTEDNESS IN CONDUCT,
HE DISREGARDED THE ORDINARY OBJECTS OF WORLDLY AMBITION,
AND SHEWED HIMSELF ON ALL OCCASIONS
THE ENEMY OF PUBLIC ABUSES,
THE FRIEND OF CIVIL AND RELIGIOUS LIBERTY,
THE OPPONENT OF OPPRESSIVE WAR,
THE PROMOTER OF PEACE,
AND THE ADVOCATE OF ALL THE CLAIMS OF HUMANITY.

"HE BEING DEAD YET SPEAKETH."

The REV. EDWARD DANIEL CLARKE, LL.D.[1], was born in 1769, and when about ten years old went to school. His progress there was not very satisfactory: he was idle and showed a want of application, which got him into scrapes with his Master. He was very athletic, and once saved his brother from drowning when they were at home for the holidays. But still he was fond of reading, and used to light a candle after every one was asleep, and read in bed. Once he set light to his bed-curtains, and would seriously have endangered the School had not the House-Master opportunely entered the room, and put out the flames. On Dr. Knox's recovery from a dangerous illness, Clarke composed and presented to him a thanksgiving ode, which, however, showed no very conspicuous talent. In 1786 he went to Jesus College, Cambridge (B.A. in 1790, and M.A. 1794), and after that commenced those travels which have rendered him so famous. At the age of twenty-eight he became a Fellow of his College; and as tutor to Mr. Cripps travelled through Europe, Asia, Egypt, and Palestine. He was instrumental in preserving the so-called sarcophagus of Alexander the Great from falling into the hands of the French, and gained it a place in the British Museum. During this time he studied Mineralogy, and on his return to England was made an LL.D. and Professor of Mineralogy in his University. Between 1810 and 1819 he published his volumes of travels, besides other books. In 1822 he died, having married whilst on his travels a daughter of Sir Thomas Rush, through whose influence he obtained the living of Harlton.

Dr. Clarke's school life.

After his University education he commenced his travels,

And studied mineralogy.

[1] Life, by Rev. William Otter. Rose's Biographical Dictionary, 1857. Nichol's Literary Anecdotes, vol. iv. p. 389. Cate's Dictionary of General Biography, 1867, p. 217.

DR. JAMES STANIER CLARKE[1], the traveller's brother, was also at school at the same time. He attended Lord Nelson, as naval chaplain, at the battle of Trafalgar, was a noted preacher in London at the Park-street and Trinity Chapels, Librarian to George IV., and Rector of Coombes, Sussex. He wrote several works, as, "The Progress of Maritime Discovery from the Earliest Period to the Close of the Eighteenth Century," also a "Life of Nelson;" and the "Naval Chronicle" originated with him. His death took place twelve years after his brother's, in 1834.

CAPTAIN GEORGE CLARKE[2], R.N., the third son, whose undaunted spirit and professional skill were well known and universally respected in the Naval Service, was brought up at Tunbridge, in the same school where Sir Sidney Smith received his education, under Dr. Knox. The openness of his heart and inflexible attachment to truth were soon remarked and valued by his Master. He was introduced to the notice of Admiral Lord Hood by the late George Medley, Esq., his godfather; and after distinguishing himself on several occasions,—and particularly whilst First Lieutenant of the Lowestoffe frigate, in an action with two French ships of superior force,—Lieut. Clarke was promoted to the rank of Commander, by Earl St. Vincent, in the Mediterranean, at the request of the late Admiral Payne. After continuing on that station for some time as Commander of L'Aurore, stationed at Gibraltar, Captain Clarke returned to England, as Commodore of Lord Nelson's prizes; and it was owing to his skill and judgment that those ships in their then tattered

Marginalia:
- Dr. J. S. Clarke was a naval chaplain,
- A great preacher,
- And a promoter of the "Naval Chronicle."
- Captain Clarke was in the navy, in which he very greatly distinguished himself
- At Gibraltar,

---

[1] Nichol's Literary Anecdotes, vol. iv. p. 387. Rose's Biographical Dictionary.
[2] Nichol's Literary Anecdotes, vol. iv. p. 392.

state ever arrived in safety: his fatigue and exertions on that occasion brought on a severe illness, under which he long laboured. During the year 1800 he was appointed by Lord Spencer to the Braakel, of 64 guns; after having Admiral Holloway's flag on board, during the summer of that year, in Portsmouth harbour, Captain Clarke was attached to the Egyptian expedition, and was particularly recommended to the notice of Admiral Lord Keith by his Royal Highness the Prince of Wales. He received a medal from the Grand Signior, a box set with diamonds, and other marks of his favour, and was afterwards sent to protect our factory at Smyrna, and to watch the secret cabals of the French in Greece. On his return to England he was ordered to fit for Admiral Russel's flag, when it was discovered that the same ship which Captain Clarke had brought from the Levant was not even safe to go round to Yarmouth. *And in Egypt.*

During the Egyptian expedition, Captain Clarke's humanity to our wounded soldiers gained him the esteem of General Sir Ralph Abercrombie and of Lord Hutchinson. At a considerable expense, and whilst himself and most of his officers were severely indisposed with the fatigue they had endured, Captain Clarke was the happy instrument of saving the lives of 350 of our wounded soldiers, who were brought from the plains of Egypt, and had been sent away by many of the other ships. This gallant officer gave them up his own cabin, ordered his lieutenants to do the same; and fed and nursed the maimed with his own hands. He then went to the Commander-in-chief, Lord Keith, and procured surgeons sufficient to attend them. On Captain Clarke's return to Europe he offered a passage in his ship *His services there.*

to the French General Le Grange, who has since commanded in the West Indies. The attention and courtesy which Le Grange thus experienced, he always declared should be returned, as they have been, should he ever take any Englishmen prisoners.

<small>His accidental death.</small> After services so truly meritorious, it is melancholy to relate that on the 1st of October, 1805, this gallant officer, with George Peters, Esq., and George Hoare, Esq., went on board Mr. Hoare's sailing-boat, with the intention of proceeding down the river, as far as Gravesend. Off Woolwich, about three in the afternoon, the sailing-boat got aground; when Captain Clarke, attended by his friend Mr. Peters, went into a small boat with a rope, in order to tow the sailing-boat afloat. This they accomplished, and had returned so near to their companions that Mr. Peters, with too much eagerness and impatience, stood up to throw the rope on board, in the act of doing which he lost his balance, and upset the boat. The current in Woolwich Reach is very strong; and the sailing-boat then making much way through the water, and refusing to come round, Mr. Hoare could lend them no assistance; oars and different articles were thrown overboard, but without effect. A collier that was passing, and saw their distress, would give them no assistance—probably, it is hoped, not being aware of the danger. Mr. Peters, unable to swim, was supported by his gallant friend Captain Clarke, who, with his well-known humanity, paid too little attention to himself: after repeated and ineffectual efforts to save Mr. Peters, Captain Clarke's strength became quite exhausted, and he was gradually seen to sink. At that awful moment a boat put off to his assistance, and saw part of the body of Captain Clarke still floating; but before they could reach the

spot, he sank with his friend to the bottom. Their bodies, after remaining four hours under water, were found, and placed during the night in the sailing-boat. On the ensuing morning they were conveyed in two hearses to the house of Mr. Peters, in Park-street, Grosvenor-square, and were buried in the church of St. Andrew, Holborn, on Tuesday, the 8th of October.

GENERAL DUMOUSTIER visited Dr. Knox as an Old Boy, in 1802, during the peace of Amiens. He was aide-de-camp to Napoleon I., and in the battle of Marengo brought up Desaix at the critical moment. In 1813, he was in command of the eighth battalion of the "Young Guard" in the French army in Germany, consisting of about 3500 foot. His school life was passed in company with Dr. Edward Clarke and his brother. General Dumoustier was aide-de-camp to Napoleon.

SIR WILLIAM SIDNEY SMITH, G.C.B., British Admiral[1], was the son of a captain in the army, John Spencer Smith, of Midgham, Sussex, and was born at Westminster, 1764. He received his education chiefly under Dr. Vicesimus Knox, of Tonbridge School; but was sent, before the age of twelve years, as midshipman on board the Sandwich, under Lord Rodney. In 1780 he became a lieutenant; in 1782, a commander; and in 1783 obtained a post rank, with the command of the Nemesis, of 28 guns. The American war having just been brought to a close, the young captain (who was not quite 20) entered the service of the King of Sweden, who presented him with the grand cross of the Order of the Sword, for the skill and energy he displayed on several occasions, particularly in an attack on a Russian flotilla, a great part of which he destroyed. Peace between Sweden and Russia again

---

[1] Cate's Dictionary of General Biography, 1867, quoted *literatim*.

threw him out of active life, and he travelled in the south of Europe. Hearing that Lord Hood had got possession of Toulon, he hastened thither, and offered his services. Soon after his arrival it was determined to evacuate the city; and the destruction of the ships of war, which could not be carried off, was entrusted to Sir Sidney, who performed the hazardous exploit with signal ability. He was now appointed to the command of the Diamond frigate, of 38 guns, in which, with a small flotilla under his direction, he greatly annoyed the enemy; but in a gallant attempt to cut out a ship at Havre in 1796, he was taken prisoner, and on pretence of having violated the law of nations, by landing assassins in France, he was confined for two years in the prison of the Temple, at Paris. At length, by the address and intrepidity of a French officer, named Philippeaux, and two of his friends, Sir Sidney's escape was somewhat mysteriously effected. By means of a forged order to the gaoler, and false passports, they escaped to Rouen, and thence in an open boat to the Channel, where they were taken up by the Argo frigate, which soon landed them at Portsmouth. In 1798 Sir Sidney sailed in the Tigre, of 80 guns, for the Mediterranean, to assume a distinct command, as commodore, on the coast of Egypt. In March, 1799, he proceeded to St. Jean d'Acre, and on the 16th, captured a French flotilla, the guns of which he employed in the defence of Acre, against Buonaparte, who invested it two days after. Many fierce contests followed, and the French repeatedly endeavoured to carry the place by storm; but the determined valour of the British commodore and his gallant band, assisted by the troops of Hassan Bey, frustrated every attempt. Buonaparte having quitted

Egypt, Sir Sidney negotiated with General Kléber for the evacuation of the country; and by a treaty signed at El Arish, in January, 1800, the return of the French was agreed to. The British government had previously announced that it would agree to no capitulation, and hostilities were recommenced by Kléber. But they nevertheless determined to abide by it. In 1801 Sir Sidney co-operated with the army sent to Egypt under Abercombie; and he was wounded in the battle which proved fatal to that gallant general. On his return to England he received a valuable sword, with the freedom of the city, from the corporation of London; and in 1802 he was returned to Parliament as member for Rochester. He was subsequently employed in the Mediterranean and in South America. On his return to England, in 1814, he was presented with the freedom of Plymouth; in the following year he was made a Knight Commander of the Bath, in 1821 full admiral, and in 1830 lieutenant-general of marines, succeeding in that post His Majesty William IV. In 1814 he endeavoured to procure, from the Congress of Vienna, the abolition of the slave trade, and a conjoint attack of the sovereigns upon the piratical states of Barbary; but his exertions proved fruitless. He then formed at Paris an association called the Anti-Piratic, which probably helped to render the subjugation of Algiers a popular measure in France, if it did not immediately lead to that event. At the close of the war Sir Sidney's services were rewarded with a pension of 1000*l.* a year. A more chivalric character than Sir Sidney Smith is not to be found among the heroes of modern times. He died at his residence in Paris, on the 26th of May, 1840, aged 76.

Acknowledgment of his services.

His exertions to repress the slave trade were unsuccessful.

A pension was granted to him.

His death.

THOMAS KNOX, D.D.

1812—1844

<small>Dr. Thomas Knox succeeded his father.</small>

DR. THOMAS KNOX succeeded his father in 1812; he was a descendant, in the maternal line, of the Rev. Thomas Roots, Master of the School 1680 to 1714. He was at school under his father, and went to Brasenose College, Oxford, returning to Tonbridge to fill his father's place at the age of twenty-eight. He did duty at Tonbridge Church for thirty-six years, and after his father's death held the living of Runwell and Ramsden Crays, in Essex. In 1819 a report was made by the Charity Commissioners on the School, and the following extract from it gives some interesting information of the state of it then:—

REPORT OF THE COMMISSIONERS ON THE EDUCATION OF THE POOR (1819).

COUNTY OF KENT: TONBRIDGE.

The Rev. Thomas Knox is the present Master of the School, who employs two assistants. The present number of boys, strictly upon the foundation, is ten, who are all day scholars, which Mr. Knox states to be above the average of the last sixty years; but according to some old lists of the boys made in the early part of the last century, which have been produced to us by the clerk of the Company of Skinners, ten does not appear to exceed the average at that earlier period. Mr. Knox, in a letter to the Commissioners, states that six has been above the average for the last four-score years. The Master is allowed by the statutes to receive boarders, the number of which is restricted by the statutes of the founder, as appears above, unless it should seem to the Skinners' Company to be convenient that he should take a larger number; he has at present thirty-two boarders by the permission of the Company. All the day scholars come as foundation boys, and he states himself to be willing to take as many as offer, without insisting upon any qualification. The boys at present on the foundation are for the most part the sons of gentlemen, or respectable tradesmen in the parish and neighbourhood. The Master does not confine the admissions to the parishioners. The applications are not numerous enough to call upon him to exercise any preference as to place. The boys receive a classical education; and the Master states that he considers them as entitled only to instruction in the dead languages by the foundation, but they are taught reading, writing, arithmetic, and the various branches of the mathematics, at a charge of one guinea per quarter. The scholars pay for the books themselves. The foundation boys or day scholars are taught with the boarders, without any distinction whatever. The School is regularly visited on the Tuesday before Whitsunday, and the persons visiting

The number of boys.

Boarders.

Day boys.

Character of the instruction.

are usually the Master and Wardens of the Skinners' Company, in whose presence the boys are examined, and rewards are dispensed according to the founder's statutes.

<small>Foundationers comprise boarders as well as day boys.</small>
It has with some appearance of propriety been observed, that it is hardly correct, according to the intention of the founder, to speak of the scholars upon the foundation in opposition to the boarders; since boarders appear to have been in the contemplation of the founder as well as day scholars. The boarders are admitted under the statutes, paying the small statutable entrance fee to the library; receiving the education provided by the endowment, and enjoying the advantages conferred upon the School by its other benefactors (the last fellow of St. John's, who was elected by the town, having been a boarder). And it deserves notice, that the Master has declared that he makes no charge to his boarders for the education they receive under the School institution. The reason of the small number of foundation scholars, strictly so called, is probably the little importance attached by the inhabitants of Tonbridge to an education simply classical for their sons, compared with the benefits of a more general, commercial, or practical instruction, especially as the education so exclusively classical, is not followed up by any considerable provision at College. If the foundation were enlarged by the application of greater funds, so as to embrace subsequent benefits to those whose education at the School was completed, there is little doubt that the accession to the School would be increased in proportion; and that the education of a much greater number was originally intended, may be inferred with some probability from the extent of accommodation which the building, which is of great age, affords.

<small>Anticipation of the increase of the School.</small>

The Master's salary does not appear to have been raised since the year 1759; the amount was fixed by the will of Sir Andrew Judd, but additions have since been made to it in the way of gratuity; and if we look to the charter as the foundation, these salaries must be considered as capable of increase at the discretion of the Company. The Master's salary.

How far the Company of Skinners are right in treating the surplus, after paying these salaries and repairs, as their own, is a question which can only be solved by a judicial decision. A difficulty in the investigation of this point may arise from the want of the deed of conveyance to the Company by Henry Fisher, recited in the Acts 14th and 31st Elizabeth, but which the Skinners' Company declare themselves, by their clerk, unable to produce. As to the state of facts, however, it may be collected with some certainty, from the recital in the said Acts of Parliament, that Henry Fisher survived Sir Andrew Judd, and as surviving joint tenant, became solely seised of all the hereditaments which Judd had intended to pass to the Company; and that he conveyed the same expressly in furtherance of the charitable objects of Sir Andrew Judd, whose confidential servant he was, to the same Company; which conveyance by Henry Fisher, and the objects of it, the statutes of the 14th and 31st Elizabeth appear by their titles and contents to have been designed to establish and confirm, *for the maintenance and benefit of the School.* Nor can it escape observation, that all the transactions, subsequent to the will of Sir Andrew Judd, treat the conveyance to the Company as meaning to pass the property to them in their corporate capacity as "Governors of the possessions, revenues, and goods of the Free Grammar School of Tonbridge." Disposal of surplus revenue.
Facts weighing upon the question.

Friday, 13*th November*, 1818.

The Rev. THOMAS KNOX.

Rev. Thomas Knox.

Are you the Master of the Free Grammar School at Tonbridge?—I am; I succeeded my father in January, 1812.

Can you give any information respecting the foundation of the School, and the property belonging to it?—I cannot, except what I learn from the papers I now produce; these are extracts from the wills of Sir Andrew Judd, the founder, and Sir Thomas Smith, a benefactor; also from the wills of persons who have bequeathed exhibitions to the School; a copy of a letter from the Skinners' Company to the parish, on the subject of Sir Thomas Smith's bequest; and the opinions of counsel upon the extent of the freedom of the School.

Have the Skinners' Company the management of the property?—They have wholly the management of it, and of all the donations relating to it.

Were you appointed by the Skinners' Company?—I was, and receive my salary from them.

The Master and Usher's salaries.

What is the salary you receive?—The salary for the Master, under Sir Andrew Judd's will, is 20*l.*; for the Usher 8*l.* Under Sir Thomas Smith's will, there is an addition of 10*l.* to the Master, and 5*l.* to the Usher; all of which is paid to me, making together a salary of 43*l.* The further sum of 42*l.* is annually voted to the Master as a gratuity, making, in the whole, 85*l.* I am required, by the will of the founder, to have an Usher; I engage him, and pay him 100*l.* a year, and one guinea a quarter for every mathematical scholar: his income last year was above 160*l.*;

he has also board, lodging, and washing. The salary I pay him includes his salary as mentioned by the will. I have also a second assistant, to whom, being a very young man, I give 25 guineas a year, and board, lodging, and washing.

I have a house and garden, rent and tax free, rated in the parish books at 40l. a year; upon which I pay for the Company the following taxes:—

	£	s.	d.
Poor's rates, 8 shillings in the pound	16	0	0
Assessed taxes	52	3	4
Highway rate, 11d. in the pound	3	16	8
Gaol rate, 1s. in the pound	2	0	0
Church rate, 6d. in the pound	1	0	0
	£75	0	0

Rates and taxes payable by the Head Master.

How many boys are there in the School upon the foundation?—Ten; they are all day scholars.

There are then no boarders on the foundation?—None; there is no provision by the statutes for boarding them; but the Master is allowed by the statutes to take boarders on his own account. *Number of boys in the School.*

How many scholars have you as boarders, who are not on the foundation?—I have at this time 32. I am allowed by the Company to take as many boarders as I choose. All who are day scholars come as foundation boys, and I am ready to take as many as choose to come. I have spoken to several inhabitants of the parish, and inquired why they did not send their children to take the advantage of the School: two of the present foundation scholars have come, as I believe, in consequence of such representation.

How are the boys appointed?—They are admitted by me, upon application made by their parents or friends.

What description of boys do you admit?—I admit any that apply.

<small>Qualification for admission.</small>

What qualifications do you require in the scholars you admit?—I receive all that apply, without requiring any qualification. The present boys on the foundation are the sons of gentlemen in the neighbourhood and respectable tradesmen. I do not restrict the admission to parishioners, the number of applicants not having ever been so great as to call upon me to make any selection or preference.

<small>Character of education.</small>

What are the advantages the foundation boys receive at your School?—A classical education in Latin and Greek, and if required, Hebrew. This is all the instruction I consider them to be entitled to under the foundation; but they are also all taught English, reading, writing, arithmetic, and the various branches of mathematics, at a charge of one guinea a quarter. There is a trifling sum of sixpence directed by the statutes to be paid by the foundation boys upon admission, which has been received in my predecessor's time, but never in mine. No books are found for the scholars; I provide such as are necessary, which are paid for by their parents. The foundation boys are taught with the boarders; I make no distinction whatever, either in or out of school hours, but encourage them to mix together.

<small>Annual Visitation.</small>

Is the School regularly visited by the Skinners' Company?—Yes, the Master and Wardens regularly visit it on the Tuesday preceding Whitsunday, at which time both boarders and foundation boys are examined in the presence of the visitors, according to the statutes. The present examiner is the Rev. William Gordon, of Speldhurst. There are Latin and Greek speeches in the morning, selected from the classical authors used in the School, and again in the evening, with the addition of English compositions, when the boys receive the rewards ordered by the founder's statutes.

Are there any exhibitions belonging to this School?—There are six, under the will of Sir Thomas Smith, at 10*l*. a year each, to any scholars from this School going to any college in either University. These I believe are all full.

Exhibitions belonging to the School.

Have these exhibitions ever received any increase?—Never.

Are there any further exhibitions?—There is one, left by Mr. Fisher, in the gift of the Skinners' Company, for the benefit of a scholar from Tonbridge School, limited to Brazen-nose College, Oxford. I received it, and think it was about 16*l*. a year, but must refer to the Company for further particulars. It is now held by a young man from this School.

An exhibition was given by the will of Mr. Lampard, of 2*l*. 13*s*. 4*d*. charged on a house and land at Lamberhurst, to a free scholar from this School to either of the Universities, to be nominated by the vicar and churchwardens. This is now vacant, but will be filled up this week. This exhibition is paid by the proprietor of the premises to the scholar himself.

Another, left by Mr. Holmden, in the first instance to a scholar from Sevenoaks School, and in default of one from thence, to a scholar from Tonbridge School, in the appointment of the Leathersellers' Company. This was 4*l*. a year; but the Company, as I understand, have, out of their own funds, made it 8*l*. This is not now held by a scholar from either School. I applied for it for a scholar from Tonbridge School: it had been then just filled; but the Company, in lieu of it, gave the scholar for whom I applied one of their own open exhibitions of 16*l*. per annum.

<small>Exhibitions belonging to the School.</small>

Sir Thomas White, the founder of St. John's College, Oxford, gave one of his fellowships to a scholar from this School, to be nominated by the " Prætores vel seniores " of the town of Tonbridge. When a vacancy takes place, we call a meeting by public notice in the church of the elder and principal inhabitants of the town, to make the nomination. This fellowship is now held by Henry Arthur Woodgate.

We find in Hasted's History of Kent mention made of an exhibition founded by a Mr. Lewis, and four others founded by Sir James Lancaster; do you know any thing of these?—No, I do not; I know of none but those I have mentioned.

Friday, 4th December, 1818.

FRANCIS GREGG, Esquire.

<small>Francis Gregg, Esq.</small>

ARE you the clerk of the Skinners' Company?—I am.

In what relation does that Company stand to the Grammar School?—As governors, appointed by Sir Andrew Judd, the founder. I produce the copy of a charter of King Edward VI., and also the translation.

[The witness produces the same.

On examining the charter, it appeared to be dated 7th Edward VI.; to contain a licence to the Company to take in mortmain, and to have a corporate name and stile, succession and the other incidents of a corporation.

The witness also produced a copy of Sir Andrew Judd's will; dated 2nd September, 1558.

The witness also produced a copy of a deed poll of Henry Fisher, with a schedule annexed; dated 30th April, 4th Elizabeth, stated in the report of this case. Documents relating to the School.

The witness produced the statutes of the School; dated 12th May, 6th Elizabeth.

The witness also produced the copy of an Act of Parliament, passed in the 14th year of Queen Elizabeth, intituled, "An Act for the further and better assurance of certain Lands, Tenements, &c., for the maintenance of the Free Grammar School of Tonbridge in the county of Kent."

The witness also produced a copy of the will of Sir Thomas Smith; dated 4th September, 1624.]

Is all the property belonging to the School comprised in the above-mentioned documents?—It is; but some of the property is applicable to other purposes than those of the School. The School property.

What is the present state of the property?—I have prepared a rental of the whole property of Sir Andrew Judd, which is here produced.

[The witness delivered in such Rental.]

What is your mode of letting the property? We usually give the tenant a preference; after our surveyor has surveyed the premises, three years before the existing leases terminate, the original tenant, or the tenant in possession is then permitted to offer for the property; if he does not, before the period of six months before the expiration of the term, come up to what we consider the real value, we open the property to public competition under advertisement. Mode of letting it.

This has not often been necessary, but it is the principle on which we act. There is a resolution of our Court on the subject, which I produce.

[The witness delivered in such resolution, of which the following is a copy:]

"29th April, 1794.

The Mode of letting it.

"Resolved, That it is the opinion of this committee, that the several lessees and their representatives, and also tenants in possession, shall be at liberty to treat for new leases when the old ones shall be within three years of expiring; but that if some of the parties interested in such leases, shall not have agreed for a new lease of the same, at the time the old lease is within six months of expiring, that then the committee of leases shall be at liberty to advertise the same in the public papers, or in any other mode that shall be deemed advisable, that they will be ready to treat at an appointed time for new leases, with any person or persons that may think proper to apply for that purpose."

Expenses of maintaining the School.

What is the expenditure of the Company for the School?—We pay all the taxes of the School, the repairs, salaries for the Master and Usher; we pay the sum of 20*l*. to the Master, and 8*l*. to the Usher, under Sir Andrew Judd's will; and we add yearly gratuities of 31*l*. 10*s*. to the Master, and 10*l*. 10*s*. to the Usher, by an annual vote of the Company. I cannot find when these gratuities began to be paid, but they have been made for several years; in the year 1759-60, I observe the payment entered in my father's account. Under Sir Thomas Smith's will we pay 10*l*. to the Master and 5*l*. to the Usher; we also pay the six exhibitions annually under his will. Under Fisher's grant we also pay an exhibition to Brazen-nose College of 18*l*. and some odd shillings; he must be both of that college and of Tonbridge School; the whole payment was 5*l*., that is, to the scholar 2*l*. 13*s*. 4*d*.; to his tutor, 13*s*. 4*d*.; to the College, 1*l*. 13*s*. 4*d*. These have all received a proportional increase.

What is the average amount of repairs?—I am not aware at this present moment, but it shall be furnished. The repairs are directed when necessary, on the visitations of the School by the Company. There is an annual visitation in the month of May. Repairs.

Are there any other fixed payments under the different donors' grants?—There are, applicable to other purposes than the School.

What becomes of the residue, after all the payments made under the will?—The residue, after the payments, and of such increased payments as the Company have thought proper to make beyond the settled payments, is carried by the Company to their own general fund. Surplus income.

Are there any regulations as to the admission of the children?—It was limited by some order of our Court, in the year 1765, to boys of Tonbridge, Speldhurst, and Bidborough, but I will supply a copy of the regulation.

Does any clergyman attend as examiner on the visitation? —Yes, and we pay three guineas annually. Examiner.

Can you state an annual average number of foundation boys educated for some years past?—I cannot; the whole premises are very spacious, and capable of accommodating a great number of boys, although of great antiquity. Considerable improvements and additions have been made by the Company from time to time.

Have you any exhibitions founded by Sir James Lancaster or a Mr. Lewis, applicable to this School?—We have Minor Exhibitions.

exhibitions founded by Sir James Lancaster and Mr. Lewis, but they are open exhibitions.

Visitors. Is there any account in your books, of any visitation of this School by All Souls' College?—I never heard of any interference on the part of that college, or any other.

Friday, 11*th December*, 1818.

FRANCIS GREGG, Esquire, re-examined.

[The Witness produced a copy of a resolution of a special court of the Skinners' Company, on 24th January, 1765, of which the following is a copy.]

At a special court of Assistants of the worshipful Company of Skinners, London, held at their hall the 24th day of January, 1765, to take into consideration the several opinions of counsel relating to the freedom of Tonbridge School, the court came to the following resolution:—

The freedom of the School in 1765. Resolved, That it is the opinion of this court that the inhabitants of the parish of Tonbridge have a right to have their children (being qualified according to the statutes of Sir Andrew Judd, the founder) instructed in grammar learning at this Company's School at Tonbridge, without paying any other consideration than sixpence each at first entrance, and answering and paying such other small penalties and forfeitures as such children may incur by disobedience to the founder's statutes while they are at School.

Ordered, That a copy of the above resolution be sent to Mr. Scoones, the vestry clerk at Tonbridge, and that another copy thereof be sent to Mr. Towers, the Master of the said School.

[The witness produced copies of the opinions of counsel relating to the freedom of Tonbridge School, which he considered to be referred to in the foregoing resolution.] *Documents relating to the School.*

[The witness produced an office copy of the Act of the 31st Eliz. intituled, "An Act for the better assurance of Lands and Tenements for the maintenance of the Free Grammar School of Tonbridge in the county of Kent."]

[The witness produced two plans, one of the ground called The Sandhills, in the parish of Saint Pancras, before it was built upon; and the other, of that part of it which has been let to Mr. Burton on a building lease, and which, as far as it extends, was found to correspond in point of dimensions with the old plan.]

[The witness produced the original articles of agreement for building leases made between the Skinners' Company and James Burton, dated 29th September, 1807, and also a copy thereof.]

Have leases been granted under this agreement equal to the amount of the rent stipulated to be paid by Mr. Burton? —Yes, they have.

[The witness produced a statement of the repairs done at Tonbridge School, of which the following is a copy.] *Amount of repairs from 1797—1818*

In 1797 expenses of repairs for Tonbridge
School, about £36
1798 180
1799 43
1800 32
1801 40
1802 113

Repairs.

1803	£108
1804	264
1805	200
1806	400
1807	294
1808	520
1809	112
1810	—
1811	163
1812	122
1813	105
1814	596
1815	735
1816	251
1817	124
1818	107
	£4,545

The chief points in the foregoing Report.

According to this Report the number of the boys was 42, of whom 10 were "foundationers," all day boys. The fixed income of the Head Master was 20*l.* from Sir Andrew Judde's will, 10*l.* from Sir Thomas Smythe's, and an annual vote from the Skinners' Company of 42*l.* Besides this, there was the house attached to the School, and the income from the boarders. The Second Master's income was about 160*l.* a year, besides board, &c., and he was aided by another master. The admission-money, which had to be paid to the common box to provide books, had been discontinued for some time; indeed Dr. Knox had no recollection of ever having heard of the actual payment during his lifetime.

It was about the year 1819 that the value of the School property began to increase so much that Dr. Knox thought himself justified in raising the question of the surplus revenues of the School, whether they should belong to the Skinners' Company or to the School exclusively. Hitherto the income of the School property had not been sufficient to defray the expenses attendant upon keeping up the School, and the deficit had been supplied by the Company. The result of this matter, about which there was for some time a lively discussion between the Head Master and the Governours, was that the Vice-Chancellor as well as the Lord-Chancellor (to whom the Company referred the Vice-Chancellor's decision) decided that the surplus revenues should be applied by the Company, in their capacity of Governours of the School, to School purposes only. A scheme, moreover, was directed to be prepared in Chancery, which finally set the question at rest, remodelled the statutes, and created four annual Exhibitions of 100*l.* a year each, to last for four years. *The question of the surplus revenues.*

THE NEW SCHEME.

INTRODUCTORY.

A SUIT having been instituted in the Court of Chancery, touching the School Estates, and the application thereof, and for the establishment of the School, by the decree made therein, dated the 16th day of March, 1820,— it was, amongst other things, referred to one of the Masters of the said Court, to approve of a Scheme for the future establishment of the Free Grammar School, having regard to the then annual rents of the School Estates. *Introduction to the New Scheme.*

Introduction to the Scheme of 1825.

By the Report of the said Master, dated the 24th day of December, 1824, he certified that, having considered the several schemes, which had been laid before him, together with the said Letters Patent and the said orders, or statutes of the said Sir Andrew Judde, he had thought it expedient and proper that the privileges of the said Free Grammar School should not only extend to boys and youths whose parents or guardians should *bonâ fide* reside within the town and parish of Tunbridge, but also to such boys and youths whose parents or guardians should reside in any other parish or place in the county of Kent, within the distance of ten miles by the ordinary roads and ways from the church of the said town of Tunbridge; which boys and youths should be considered as constituting the first class; and, that there might be a sufficient number of youths to receive the exhibitions thereinafter mentioned, he had thought it proper and advisable that there should be another, or second class, comprehending all boys and youths of the united Kingdom of Great Britain, who, being qualified under the regulations thereinafter mentioned, should be capable of receiving the said Exhibitions: and the said Master further certified, that he had thought it requisite and proper to alter and enlarge several of the said orders of the said Sir Andrew Judde, and that certain other of the orders of the said Sir Andrew Judde appeared to him to be inapplicable, or unnecessary for the future government of the said School: and the said Master being of opinion that Exhibitions for youths going from the said School to one of the Universities of Oxford or Cambridge, might be most beneficially established, he had prepared such articles as appeared to him to be necessary for effectuating that purpose, and also such other new articles, as from the then present circumstances appeared to him to be necessary for the future government and establishment of the said Free Grammar School, and that the several articles thereinafter set forth in his said Report formed, and he had approved of the same as, a proper scheme for the future establishment of the said Free Grammar School, from Christmas, 1824, having regard to the then annual rents of the said School Estates.

By the order of the Lord High Chancellor, dated the 18th of July, 1825, it was directed, that the aforesaid Report as to the scheme for the future establishment of the Free Grammar School at Tunbridge should be varied in certain articles of the same scheme, and that the scheme for the establishment of such Free Grammar School should be, and consist of the several articles thereinafter mentioned, reserving at all times to the Skinners' Company, they taking the advice of All Souls' College, in the University of Oxford, the power to make such regulations respecting the said Free Grammar School, as, having relation to the plan thereby directed to be carried into execution, are not inconsistent with the said plan; and also such regulations as, having no relation to the said plan, the said Company had authority to make, prior to the institution of the said suit, the same being made with the advice of the said College, where it was requisite for the Company to act with such advice, and without it, where such advice was not necessary, as in the said order is mentioned. *The revision of the Statutes in accordance with the New Scheme.*

The following SCHEME, which incorporates, with some variations, the Statutes of the Founder, and retains much of their language, was finally settled, under the above order of the Court of Chancery, for the future establishment of the School.

<small>The present Statutes.</small>

I. That the Master of the said School be whole of body, well reported, Master of Arts in degree, if it may be, chosen by the Company of Skinners of London, to whose direction the Founder committed the governance of his said School and order, always foreseen that the School-master and Usher teach the Grammar approved by the King or Queen's Majesty, and that the School-master be first allowed by the Ordinary, and by examination found meet, both for his learning and dexterity in teaching, as also for his honest conversation, and for right understanding of God's true religion, set forth by public authority, whereunto he shall stir and move his scholars, and also shall prescribe to them such sentences of Holy Scripture, as shall be most expedient to induce them to godliness.

II. That the Master always appoint and elect the Usher as often as the place shall be void, whom, so appointed and presented to the said Company of Skinners, they are to admit, not knowing sufficient cause to refuse him.

III. That the Master and Usher have their houses and wages during their lives, not sufficiently convicted to have neglected their office; and if it shall happen that either of them be so convicted at any time, yet that he be not straightly removed, but gently warned and admonished, and so for the second time; and that then, if after the second admonition he do not amend and diligently follow his office and charge in the School, that he, so offending, be utterly expulsed and removed, and another to be received into his room, and to be done with all diligence by the said Company of Skinners.

IV. That the Master and Usher shall neither of them be a common gamester and haunter of taverns; nor by any extraordinary or unnecessary expenses in apparel, or otherwise, become an infamy to the School, and an evil example to the young, to whom, in all points, they ought to show themselves an example of an honest, continent, and godly behaviour. *The present Statutes.*

V. If it happen that the Master or Usher be visited with a common disease, as the ague, or any other curable sickness, that he, so visited, be tolerated for the time, and his wages fully allowed, so that his office be discharged by his sufficient deputy; but if they or any of them fall into any infectious or incurable disease, especially through their own evil behaviour, then, that he, so infected, be removed and put away, and another to be chosen in his room.

VI. If it happen that the Master or Usher, after long time spent in the School, do wax impotent, and unable, through age, or other infirmities, to endure the travail and labour necessary in the School, that he be favourably borne withal, so that his office be satisfied by his sufficient deputy, although he himself be not present.

VII. That the Master or Usher be at liberty to remain single, or to marry, or to take priesthood, so that he trouble not himself with any care or worldly business that might hinder his office in the School.

VIII. That if any controversy happen to arise or grow between the Master and Usher at any time, that they then refer the whole matter to the Master and Wardens of the Company of Skinners in London, and to their successors; and they do stand to their order and determination in the same, upon pain of deprivation from their office.

IX. If there happen to be such contagious sickness as the plague, or such like, that the School cannot continue, yet, nevertheless, both the Master and Usher shall have their wages fully paid, being always in readiness to teach as soon as God shall make such contagious sickness to cease.

X. If it shall happen that the Master or Usher shall die at any time in their office, their executors or administrators shall receive so much money as for his or their service was due, at the hour of his or their death, and in such case the room to be supplied with as much convenient speed as may be; and, for the vacant time, the survivor to satisfy for the whole charge, and to receive so much as is due for the time.

XI. That the Master keep a Register, and in the same write the name and surname of every scholar at his entering; and that the same Master of the same School shall make a just and true account to the said Master and Wardens of Skinners, or two of them, yearly, of all such scholars as shall have been received into the School, and the names of such as shall have departed thence, so that a true account may be kept thereof.

XII. Acknowledging God to be the only author of all knowledge and virtue, it is declared by the said Sir Andrew Judde, that the Master and Usher of the School, with their scholars, at seven of the clock, do first, devoutly kneeling on their knees, pray to Almighty God, according to the form to be by the Master prescribed.

XIII. That the Master, twice in a month at least, examine those that be under the Usher's hands, to understand how they profit, and go forward in their learning.

The present Statutes.

XIV. That the Usher practise and use such order and form in teaching as the Master shall think good.

The present Statutes.

XV. That all the Scholars, upon Sabbaths and Holydays, resort in due time to divine service in the Parish Church of Tunbridge, the Master and Usher, or one of them at the least, being present to oversee them, and that the Master and Usher do duly, every Monday in the morning, call to reckoning all such of his Scholars as shall either absent themselves from the Church, or come tardy to it, or otherwise use themselves not reverently there in praying, every one of them having a Prayer Book, in Latin, or English, according to the said Master's appointment.

XVI. Considering that virtue and knowledge by praise and reward are in all estates maintained and increased, and especially in youth, it is declared by the said Sir Andrew Judde, that in every year, once, to wit on the day of the visitation of the School hereinafter appointed, there be kept in this School disputations upon questions provided by the Master, from One of the Clock at Afternoon, till Evensong time, at which disputation the Master is to desire the Vicar of the town, with one or two others of knowledge, or more, dwelling nigh, to be present in the School, if it please them to hear the same :—the disputations ended, to determine, which three of the whole number have done best by the judgment of the Master and learned hearers, and that the first allowed have a Pen of Silver, whole of gilt ; the second, a Pen of Silver, parcel gilt ; the third, a Pen of Silver, for their rewards ; and that the whole company go in order decently, by two and two, into the Parish Church, the three Victors to come last next to the Master and Usher, each of them having a garland upon their heads provided for the purpose; and in the Church, then and there to kneel, or stand in some convenient place, to be approved by the discretion of the Wardens and Master of the School, and to say or sing some Psalms, or Hymns, with a Collect, for the preservation of the King's or Queen's Majesty, and to have some honourable remembrance of their Founder, so to be appointed and devised by the Master.

The present Statutes.

XVII. That it shall not be lawful for the Master or Usher, or any of their friends, at going away from their office, to spoil beforehand, or take away from thence, any such things as are set up and fastened in their house or houses, and planted in their orchards or gardens, but freely to leave the same with as good will as for their time they have enjoyed the use thereof.

XVIII. That the Company of Skinners have an Inventory in their hands of all things that appertain unto the School, be they books, or implements in the Master's or Usher's house, so that at the departing they may be staysd to the School's behalf.

XIX. That there shall be truly written, word for word, two copies of these ordinances, the one ever to remain in the hands of The Skinners, the other in the custody of the Master of the said School; or, at such time as the Master's place is vacant, to remain in the Usher's hands, so that they both may thereby learn what appertaineth to their office, and also that on their admission they shall promise, before honest witnesses, to keep and see executed all such points as concern them and their scholars, to the uttermost of their power, during all the time that they remain in the office.

XX. That both the Master and Usher shall endeavour themselves to the continual profiting of all the said scholars of the said Grammar School, and of their parts faithfully observe and keep all the points and articles hereinbefore and hereinafter contained, as by the same orders more plainly doth and may appear; and finally, if the said Master or Usher shall manifestly neglect or break any such orders, being thereof twice admonished by the said Master and Wardens, Governors aforesaid, and, notwithstanding, continue the breach thereof, that then it shall be lawful to the said Master and Wardens, Governors aforesaid, to expel and put out the party so offending, and to place another able man in his room or office.

XXI. That the house and buildings for the Master of the said School shall be made to accommodate, and shall be maintained in a state fit for the accommodation of his family and scholars; and that a suitable house and building shall be provided and maintained for the Usher, his family, and scholars.

XXII. That the Master of the said School shall not take, or board, diet, or lodge in his house, or rooms, above the number of sixty scholars, inclusive of the twelve scholars mentioned in the sixth original order of Sir Andrew Judde; and that the Usher shall not take above the number of forty scholars, inclusive of the eight scholars mentioned in the said sixth original order of Sir Andrew Judde, unless it shall seem convenient to the Company of Skinners that

The present Statutes

the said Master and Usher, upon occasion, may have a greater number at board and lodging with them.

> The present Statutes.

XXIII. That no boy be admitted into the School who shall not, at the time of the application for admission, be of the age of eight years.

XXIV. That no boy be admitted into the said School who shall not, previously thereto, be able to write competently, and read English perfectly; and the Master of the said School, for the time being, shall examine every proposed scholar, and admit him, if he shall be so qualified, but not otherwise.

XXV. That no boy shall be allowed to continue in the said School after he shall have completed the nineteenth year of his age.

XXVI. That any housekeeper of the town of Tunbridge shall be permitted to receive not exceeding thirty boys as boarders, who shall be scholars of the said free Grammar School, provided such inhabitant shall obtain from the said Governors a written licence for that purpose, upon the production of testimonials from the Master as to the moral character and fitness of the applicant for the charge of such boarders, and that the said licence be renewed annually by the said Governors.

XXVII. That the salary of twenty pounds, given to the Master by the said Sir Andrew Judde, be increased to the sum of five hundred pounds per annum, clear of all deduction; and that the salary given by the said Sir Andrew Judde to the Usher be increased to the sum of two hundred pounds per annum, clear of all deductions; the said salaries to be paid half-yearly, at Christmas and Midsummer, by the said Governors, out of the rents of the said estates; such respective salaries to commence from Midsummer-day, one thousand eight hundred and twenty-four.

<small>The present Statutes.</small>

XXVIII. That the annual sum of seven pounds ten shillings be paid by every boy, who shall not be in the first of the aforesaid two classes described in the Master's Report, to the Master, and the annual sum of three pounds to the Usher, for his instruction at the said School; such payments to be respectively made by the parents or guardians of the said boys.

XXIX. That the sixteen Exhibitions of one hundred pounds a year each be founded, as part of the Establishment of the said School, for the boys thereof, who shall go off to the University of Oxford or Cambridge, under the regulations hereinafter set forth.

XXX. That such boys as shall be of the first class of scholars, and shall be duly qualified to receive such Exhibitions, shall be preferred to those of the second class.

XXXI. That the boys now in the School, whether above or under nineteen years of age, who shall respectively be applicants to go off to College upon the said Exhibitions prior to Christmas one thousand eight hundred and twenty-nine, shall, in case such boys respectively shall, at the time of such application, have been five years in the said School, immediately after such application, be examined by such person or persons as the Governors shall appoint; and, if found duly qualified, such boys shall respectively be thereupon presented by the Governors to such Exhibitions, provided that a number not exceeding two be presented in any one year.

The present Statutes.

XXXII. That until Christmas one thousand eight hundred and twenty-nine, the said Governors shall appoint an Examiner to attend at the Annual Visitation, for the purpose of examining all the boys in the School.

XXXIII. That upon the Annual Visitation, from and after Christmas one thousand eight hundred and twenty-nine, an Examiner shall be appointed by the Governors for the examination of the boys and youths, who shall be candidates for the said Exhibitions.

XXXIV. That the said Examiner shall be of not less than seven years' standing at, and a resident Member of, one of the Universities of Oxford or Cambridge, and have taken the degree of Master of Arts, or Bachelor of Civil Law, and that application be made by the said Governors to the Warden and Fellows of the College of All Souls', Oxford, to nominate such Examiner, if the said Warden and Fellows shall think fit.

XXXV. That the said Examiner do, on every Annual Visitation, publicly examine all the boys and youths in the said School, to ascertain their progress in learning.

XXXVI. That the said Examiner shall subsequently examine in the School-room all such boys and youths as shall become Candidates for Exhibitions, and shall report to the Governors and Master respectively, the names of all such of the said last-mentioned boys and youths in the said classes respectively, as he shall find qualified to stand for Exhibitions.

XXXVII. That the said Examiner shall in such Report arrange the names of the said Candidates in the said respective classes, according to their respective excellence in classical learning.

XXXVIII. That from and after Christmas one thousand eight hundred and twenty-nine, the said Governors shall yearly present, or give, at their said Visitation, the Exhibitions to any four of the boys and youths of the said first class, who shall be reported by the said Examiner as qualified for the same; and in case there shall not be found in the said first class boys and youths qualified as aforesaid for an University education, to receive the said four Exhibitions, then the said Governors shall present or give all, or so many of the said annual Exhibitions as the boys and youths in the first class shall not receive, to any of the boys and youths of the second class, who may be reported by the said Examiner as qualified to receive such Exhibitions.

XXXIX. That the said Examiner shall be paid the sum of fifteen pounds fifteen shillings; and also the further sum of fifteen pounds fifteen shillings for his travelling and other expenses; and that such payments shall be provided for by the said Governors out of the said Estates.

XL. That the said Exhibitions shall be held by the said Exhibitioners for four years, from the commencement of the University Term next after the presentation of such Exhibitioner, and for such portion of the said four years only, as they shall be *bonâ fide* resident at one of the Universities during the usual Terms; and in case any of the said Exhibitions shall cease before the expiration of such period as aforesaid, then the said Exhibitions, for the residue of the said period, shall be given by the Governors of the said School, for the time being, to any youths then or formerly members of the said School, who shall have undergone the aforesaid examinations, and proved themselves qualified for the Exhibitions, although they failed in obtaining the same, and who shall be then resident Members of one of the said Universities, and be under the degree of Bachelor of Arts; always preferring the youths of the first class to those of the second class.

XLI. That it appearing from the list of boys and youths now of the said School, and of the times of their entrance, that a small number only can be qualified to be candidates for the said Exhibitions prior to Christmas one thousand eight hundred and twenty-nine, and that the full number of Exhibitions intended to be hereby established cannot, at the soonest, be filled until four years from that period; the unappropriated surplus funds, and the surplus of the general account of the rents of the said Estates, shall, from time to time, be applicable to the expense which will attend the alterations and repairs of the said house of the Master, and of that intended for the Usher, and of the School-room and other buildings, and of the garden and other grounds to be enjoyed therewith respectively, and the purchase of suitable books for a library, and increase of the number of Exhibitions or rewards to the said Exhibitioners, who may distinguish themselves at either of the said Universities, or for the establishment of other branches of classical education, or for any other purposes for the better establishment of the said School, as the Court shall, from time to time, think proper to order and direct; and that for the purposes aforesaid, the said Governors, or any persons interested in the said School, are to be at liberty to apply to the Court as they may be advised.

XLII. That all the Assistant Masters, which may be necessary for the boys of the second class, shall be provided by the Master, and be paid by him and the Usher, in the proportions of their respective salaries. _{The present Statutes.}

XLIII. That in case the scholars of the said School, belonging to the first class, shall amount to the number of forty, there shall be provided, at the expense of the said Estates, one Assistant Master, to assist in the education of such boys, and so an additional Assistant Master shall be provided for every additional twenty scholars, unless it shall appear to the Skinners' Company, with the advice of All Souls' College, that an Assistant Master should be appointed for a less number of scholars in the first class than forty.

XLIV. That every such Assistant Master requisite for the boys of the first class, shall be a member of the established religion of England; and, if such can be obtained, shall have taken a degree at either of the Universities of Oxford or Cambridge.

XLV. That the said Master shall have the appointment and removal of all Assistant Masters, subject always to the visitatorial power of the Governors.

XLVI. That every Assistant Master shall be at liberty to take boys, scholars of the said School, as boarders in his house, not exceeding twenty in number.

XLVII. That the salary of every such Assistant Master shall not exceed eighty-four pounds per annum.

XLVIII. That a sum not exceeding twenty pounds per annum be allowed to the Master for supplying the School-room with coals.

XLIX. That the annual sum of two hundred pounds be allowed to the Governors for the expenses of the visitation of the said School.

L. That neither the Master, Usher, or Assistant Masters of the said School, shall absent themselves therefrom, except at the periods of, and during the vacation.

LI. That Rules and Regulations, as to the hours of attendance in the School of the Master, Usher, and Assistant Masters, and boys, or youths, and the fixed holidays to be given, shall be submitted by the Master of the said School to the said Governors, during the recess at Christmas one thousand eight hundred and twenty-four, who are, before the expiration of such recess, to settle the same; and such Governors are, from time to time thereafter, to alter or vary such Rules or Regulations, as circumstances may require, and, in the settlement of such Rules and Regulations, and in any subsequent alteration, or variation thereof, the said Governors are to have regard to the twentieth and twenty-first articles in the Statutes of Sir Andrew Judde, in the said Report set forth, and the general purpose of the Founder as therein expressed.

LII. That the said Rules and Regulations, when settled by the said Governors, and as the same shall be, from time to time, altered or varied by them, as in the next preceding Article is mentioned, shall be considered as, and be part of the scheme for the future establishment of the said free Grammar School, and shall be, from time to time, added to the other Articles herein set forth, as forming the scheme for the future establishment of the said School, and the future conduct and government thereof, and the same shall be printed with such other Articles as is mentioned in the next or following Article. <small>The present Statutes.</small>

LIII. That the Governors do provide printed copies of the Articles approved for the future government of the said School, to be distributed at their said Annual Visitation in the said School.

LIV. That instead of the Annual Visitation of the Governors, as directed by the twenty-seventh original Order of the said Sir Andrew Judde, being on the first or second day after May-day, it shall hereafter be held on the Tuesday next preceding the day on which the summer vacation in each year is appointed to commence.

ADDITIONAL RULES AND REGULATIONS SETTLED BY THE GOVERNOURS IN 1844, VIZ.—

I. That the Master, and Usher, and such Assistant Masters as may be hereafter appointed, and all the scholars of the said School, shall daily attend at the School from Lady-day to the 5th of November at a quarter before seven o'clock, and from the 5th of November till Lady-day at half-past seven o'clock in the morning; and prayers being read on their first entrance into the School, according to the 12th Article, they shall continue in the School till half-past eight o'clock. <small>Additional Statutes.</small>

II. That after breakfast, the Master, and Usher, and Assistant Masters, and all the scholars, shall return to the School at half-past nine, and shall continue therein until half-past twelve o'clock on whole school-days, and until one o'clock on half-holidays.

Additional Statutes.

III. That on whole school-days, the Master, and Usher, and Assistant Masters, and all the scholars, shall return to the School after dinner at two o'clock in the afternoon, and shall continue therein till four o'clock, and that then prayers shall be read according to the form to be by the Master prescribed.

IV. That the Master, and Usher, and all Assistant Masters, shall remain in the School, diligently teaching, reading, and interpreting, during the several hours and times above prescribed; and that neither the Master, Usher, or any Assistant Master shall depart or be absent from the School during such hours or times without urgent and sufficient cause, and that in anywise either the Master or Usher shall be present always.

V. That the Master shall be at liberty to give twelve holidays in the course of the year, the following to form part of the same, viz. the Founder's Day, the King's Birthday, and the Gunpowder Plot.

VI. That a certificate of the entry and admission of every boy into the School, in the form subjoined, be forwarded to the Governors by the Master of the School on the same day, or following day, at farthest, to that on which such entry and admission take place, viz.:—

To the Master and Wardens of the Skinners' Company, Governors of Tunbridge School.

This is to certify that   aged   years, son of
                    and   of   in the county
of   was this day entered and admitted a scholar of
Tunbridge School as a   boy.

Dated this   day of   18   .

Signed,

Master.

VII. That no boy leave the School before the day and time appointed by the Master for the commencement of the Christmas, Easter, and Midsummer holidays, except upon urgent and unavoidable necessity, and with permission from the Master under his own signature. Additional Statutes.

VIII. That no boy remain away from the School after the day appointed for his return by the Master, except in case of illness or unavoidable necessity, of which notice must have been given to the Master, as the active duties of the School will commence on the next day.

IX. That during the half-year no boy be absent from the School without the especial permission of the Master; and that a written notice be given to the Master by the parent or guardian of every boy whenever absence from School may be required.

X. That all instances of disregard of the above orders be reported to the Governors, who may direct that the half-year in which the offence shall be committed shall not be allowed to form part of the five years necessary to qualify a boy to become a candidate for an Exhibition.

XI. That no boy, after his admission into the School, shall be permitted to be absent from the same, except at the stated periods of the holidays, unless prevented by illness, of which a certificate, signed by a medical attendant, must be sent to the Master, under the penalty of his being disqualified from becoming a candidate for an Exhibition.

XII. That the vacations be at three periods of the year, viz. at Christmas, Easter, and Midsummer; that the Christmas holidays do commence on the Thursday before Christmas Day, and that the boys do return on that day four

<small>Additional Statutes.</small> weeks; that the Easter holidays do commence on the day before Good Friday, and that the boys do return on that day two weeks; that the Midsummer holidays do commence on the last Thursday in July, and that the boys do return on that day six weeks.

XIII. That in all cases of extreme impropriety of conduct on the part of any boy, which may in the opinion of the Master render it advisable to expel the boy from the School, the Master shall in the first instance have the power of suspending him from attending in the School, and after reporting the case to the Governors, shall with their sanction proceed to expulsion.

XIV. That the gilt, parcel gilt, and silver pens be awarded to the three boys who shall, in the judgment of the Examiner, have done best in the production of Greek verses, Latin verses, or Latin essays, so that no one boy may receive more than one of the pens as a prize at the same visitation, in accordance with the Statutes. All other prizes (except those given by the Master of the School) to be awarded by the Governors according to the respective merits of the boys as reported by the Examiner.

<small>The difference between the original Statutes and the present ones.</small> The substance of the difference between these Statutes and the original ones is chiefly:—

I. The increase of the Head Master's income from 62l. to 500l. a year, and the provision of a separate house for the second Master.

II. The increase of the number of boarders allowed to be taken by the Head Master from twelve to sixty, and by the second Master from eight to forty; and no one could open a boarding-house in the town for more than thirty boys.

III. "Non-foundationers" were to pay ten guineas for tuition, and "foundationers" were to have the preference in receiving exhibitions.

IV. Four Exhibitions of 100*l.* a year, each tenable for four years, at Oxford or Cambridge, for all boys under nineteen years of age, who had been five years at the School [1].

V. The appointment of an Examiner to award these Exhibitions and examine the whole School for a fee of thirty guineas.

VI. Any Master was allowed to receive twenty boarders.

VII. The Governours were allowed 200*l.* for the expenses of their visitation, which was for the future to take place on the Tuesday before the last day of the Midsummer term; and copies of the Statutes were to be provided for distribution on that day among the School.

VIII. The School hours were altered thus:—Morning School, from 6.45 (in winter from 7.30) to 8.30. After breakfast from 9.30 to 12.30 (1 o'clock on half-holidays). Afternoon School was from 2 to 4 o'clock. The holidays were to be, at Christmas, from St. Thomas's Day for six weeks from the following Monday, unless St. Thomas's Day fell on a Monday, in which case, six clear weeks from that Monday. At Midsummer, the limit was six weeks from Midsummer Day, unless it fell on a Monday, when the same provision was made as at Christmas.

---

[1] Rev. J. S. West, of Winchelsea, was the first boy elected to one of these Exhibitions. He was examined at Skinners' Hall by the Rev. Dr. Rice, and went in 1825 to Jesus College, Cambridge. From 1828 to 1862 these four were reduced to three, to defray the debt incurred by the School with the Company for the repairs and enlargement of the School buildings.

IX. The Head Master was at liberty to give twelve extra holidays in the year, including the reigning Sovereign's birthday, the Gunpowder Plot, and the Founder's day (September 4th).

These alterations were made to place the School on a more modern footing, as suited the times, to give it the benefit of its enlarged revenue, and to increase the number of boys. The additional rules made in 1844 have reference to the admission and leave of absence of the boys, the terms of expulsion, the holidays, and the prizes.

Alteration and enlargement of the building.

In 1826, in consequence of the increased funds at the disposal of the Governours for School purposes, and the representations of Dr. Knox as to the want of room for the boys, the Lower School was built. The trees and the wall in front of the School were removed, and iron railings substituted. In 1827, the library, built in 1750 by Mr. Cawthorne and the Skinners' Company, was enlarged to its present size, and made to correspond externally with the other newly built wing. The old dining-hall, built in 1676, was at the same time pulled down, and a new one added, with dormitories over it.

Some personal recollections of Dr. T. Knox.

The following recollections of Dr. Knox, as far as page 187, is the kind answer of two Old Boys[1] to a request for some information about their times :—Our road brought us to the old "Rose and Crown," whose faded glories are not yet forgotten, when thirty-two four-horsed coaches passed and repassed every day, giving an air of life and bustle to the old town, which forms an agreeable contrast to its present quietness. Mine host, old Parker, then dispensed the

[1] J. F. Wadmore and Rev. H. R. Wadmore.

hospitalities of this good old inn: and having ordered dinner, we walked up with my father to see Dr. Knox. Much in awe of this respected personage, we found him in his garden, and he took us over the School and grounds. Well do I remember his fine and portly figure, his shaggy eyebrows and bright eye, and on my father saying his boys had brought their bats, the Doctor remarked, "Yes, quite right, quite right; I never knew a boy worth any thing who was not fond of cricket." At this time there were about a hundred boys in the School—it had fallen to a low ebb, in consequence of Dr. Knox having taken a prominent part in the leading events of the time, and the settlement of the great question of reform; and his attendance and speech at a great meeting at Penenden Heath, had give much offence to many. Under the Statutes the School should have commenced on a Thursday, but this rule was relaxed, and although my father sent us back on that day, School did not recommence until Monday, and the majority of the boys returned on Saturday. After the departure of my father to town, we had still two days before us, and with the instructions and under the guidance of a schoolboy, we went down town and proceeded to purchase knives, plates, spoons, forks, saucepans, teacups, and teapots, it being the custom for each boy to find and take care of his own, and to provide himself with tea, coffee, and milk, &c., as we were only provided by the Doctor with bread and butter for breakfast and tea.

 At dinner-time it was a cheerful sight to see the Doctor enter the hall, when the boys were assembled, with his hat on, his black Tommy—a short knotty, holly stick, with a grotesque head carved at one end and tapering away at the other—under his arm, wearing a silk handker-

[marginal note: The number of boys then in the School.]

chief for an apron. He was closely followed by Best, his butler, more portly than his master, short, fat, and stumpy, with little twitching eyes deeply set in his head, bearing in his hand a large joint, and behind him came Killick and others with vegetables, &c.

Dr. Knox occasionally gave "Remedies."

Occasionally it was his wont to enter into the schoolroom about ten o'clock in the morning or four o'clock on fine afternoons, and having informed the boys that he was well satisfied with the work either of the fifth or sixth forms, take a new cricket-ball from his capacious pocket, and throw it into the centre of the School, as a signal that it was a let-out or a holiday, and with a shout the boys would make for the door and rush out into the field for a game of cricket. In the autumn months, hockey was the favourite game. Hockey-cutting on half-holidays was a glorious treat; tramping through the wood and selecting the best formed sticks, and cutting them off with a bill; this, however, was not always practicable, as the noise made in cutting the tree frequently called attention to the fact that a trespass was being committed. Then came a "chivey" over the fields and across the country; but rarely, if ever, were any boys caught, as they always outstripped their enraged pursuers, bringing the sticks off in triumph, which were dried in the chimney of the Upper School after being steamed and bent to the required shape.

The work in the different forms.

There were six monitors, who read prayers in turn every morning and evening. The work, generally, in the sixth was Sophocles, Thucydides, Æschylus, Horace, Virgil. The Head Boy selected the passages for composition, and the Doctor chose the subject for the verses and theme. In the fifth, the books used were Herodotus, Cicero, and Horace;

in the fourth, Sallust, Virgil, and a little Anacreon; in the third, Greek fables, Cornelius Nepos, Virgil; in the upper second, Ovid and Cæsar, with Greek grammar; in the lower second, Latin fables and Eutropius, in both cases Ellis's Exercises; in the first, Latin grammar and English. The Doctor took the sixth and fifth forms. The Rev. Thomas Browne taught the fourth and third forms, using a cane or stick for the purpose of castigation. Mr. Hepton (familiarly called "Mazzard"), who lived in the School-house, took the upper and lower second; Mr. Moody, since Vicar of St. Nicholas, Newcastle, taught the juniors. The Latin exercises of the fifth and sixth were looked over by the Rev. E. Vinall, who was curate of the parish church, and is now Incumbent of St. John's Church at Hildenborough, in the parish of Tonbridge; he also taught these forms mathematics in the new (or lower) School, where the Doctor heard his classes say their lessons. On Sundays the elder boys read Bishop Tomline's "Introduction to the Study of the Bible," and the juniors repeated some lessons for Mr. Moody. No Greek Testament was used—indeed, religious instruction was of a very limited character. The tone of the School was altogether classical, as it is still. There was a French Master, an old French officer, who taught mathematics and French. Subsequently another French Master was appointed, whose name was Tolmar, a very kind, genial, gentlemanly man, who, doing better than his predecessor, gathered about eighteen or twenty boys together into a class. Punishment, when made use of, was almost always corporal. The unheard-of punishment of writing out 500 lines of Homer was once given by the Doctor, who caught a boy, *flagrante delicto*, riding his favourite heifer round the cricket-field!

The work in the different forms.

It was in the severe winter of 1835-6, when the frost continued to cover the ground with snow and the ponds with ice, that an arrangement was made for the boys to enjoy the exercise of skating on the lake at Summer Hill, by taking all the half-holidays of the term consecutively, on condition that as soon as the frost broke up School should be resumed during the remainder of the term without any intermission for half-holidays. For a whole month, day after day, the boys skated, and at the termination of the frost the arrangement was adhered to—but for three weeks only; the restriction was too much for Masters and boys, and by mutual consent the half-holidays were resumed.

Continuous holidays for skating.

In 1838, the field behind the School was partially levelled, by the care of the Head Master, to make the present cricket-ground; and this inscription on a brass plate, let into the stump of an old tree, still commemorates the fact [1], "Hanc aream æquandam curavit Thomas Knox, S.T.P., hujus Scholæ Magister, A.D. 1838." Previous to 1838, the annual cricket matches played by the School were two only; but two looked forward to, enjoyed, and remembered as much as or more than the twenty or so now annually played. One was against the town and the other against the old boys. Russell was the great slow bowler against the School, and his friend Waite, who always played in top-boots, was one of the stoutest and steadiest, if not most agile, batsmen on the side of the town, who used to muster in strong force as spectators. Killick, whose face, as School porter, is familiar to every old Tonbridge boy since 1826, can still remember how the present second eleven ground was the scene of many

The annual cricket matches.

---

[1] At any rate the inscription *should* be there, though it has lately disappeared from its place.

a rough and hard fought struggle of old. There was the Doctor on horseback taking a hearty interest in the game; there were the townspeople sitting in groups on the slopes, smoking their pipes and drinking the barrels of beer and cyder, which were placed under the trees that line the south side of the ground. Then at one o'clock the two elevens and the whole School used to adjourn to the dining-hall and dine together. The Doctor would then call upon one of the opposite eleven, Parker, the worthy innkeeper, or the three Coombers, famous for their glee singing, to give a song. It was one of the merriest days of the year for the School, and no one apparently enjoyed it more than the Doctor himself, who not unfrequently would sing them "The Brave Old Oak" or "Old English Gentlemen."

Dr. Knox died suddenly in 1843 at the age of fifty-nine. He was performing Divine service one Sunday in his parish church, and had retired to change his robes previous to preaching, when he was seized with a fit, carried out of the church, and shortly afterwards expired. The Latin inscription on the monument erected to his memory in Tonbridge Church, enumerates his virtues and describes his death:— *Dr. Knox's death.*

H. S. E.

THOMAS KNOX, S.T.P.

Parochiæ hujus per annos xxxvi minister,
Ecclesiarum Runwell et Ramsden-Crays
In agro Essexiensi rector,
Scholæ Tunbridgiensis primum alumnus dein magister.
Reditus fundatoris ampliores
Proprio opere feliciter recuperavit.

The Latin inscription on his tablet in Tonbridge church.

Ille hâc in æde
Cum vestes sacerdotales indueret
Divinum officium celebraturus
Repentinâ morte præreptus est
X KAL SEXT A.D. MDCCCXLIII ætatis LIX.
Vir si quis alius desideratissimus,
Præceptor indefessus,
Auctoritatem mansuetudine ita temperavit,
Ut discipulos miris modis
Sibi devinceret.
Concionator voce plenâ et canorâ,
Ardens, eloquens, nervosus,
Et vere Christianus,
Indulgentiâ in liberos,
Largitate in egenos,
Misericordiâ in calamitosos,
Comitate in vicinos,
Benevolentiâ in omnes
Commemorabilis,
In publicis rebus ut in suis
Diligens et utilissimus.

Uxorem duxit
Francescam Gul: F: Woodgate de Somerhill-arvis filiam,
Eheu immature extinctam
A.D. MDCCCXXXI,
Et in eodem sepulchro conditam,
Quam omni laude dignissimam
Unice dilexit.

JAMES IND WELLDON, D.C.L.

1843

DR. WELLDON succeeded Dr. Knox in 1843. He was a Fellow of St. John's College, Cambridge, and took his degree of B.A. in 1834, when he was in the first class in both classics and mathematics. He then became a private tutor in the University, and afterwards, for a short while, was Second Master of Oakham Grammar School. In 1836, the Second Mastership of Shrewsbury School being vacant, he was presented by St. John's College to that appointment, and thereby, in accordance with the Statutes of his College, was compelled to vacate his Fellowship. Dr. Welldon stayed at Shrewsbury for more than seven years; at first, when the late Dr. Samuel Butler, Bishop of Lichfield, was Head Master, and afterwards with Dr. Kennedy. At this time, 1843, there were only about forty-three boys in the School. The increase, however, was very large and sudden, as many as twenty-five fresh entries a term being made between 1844 and 1845. The

Dr. Welldon at Cambridge,

At Oakham.

At Shrewsbury,

At Tonbridge.

School list in 1844 shows 107 names on it; in 1854, 141; and in 1869, 197.

Rev. E. I. Welldon.

The Rev. Edward Ind Welldon followed his brother to the School in 1844 as Assistant Master. He was a prizeman and Foundation Scholar in 1841 of Queens' College, Cambridge; he took his degree of B.A. in 1844, and in 1851 was elected Fellow of his College. In 1855 he took the place of the Rev. Thomas Brown at Tonbridge, who had been for many years Second Master, and transferred his boarding-house to Judde House, adjoining the School on the north side. He has the general supervision of the Lower School, and takes the "Suspension" (a form between the third and fourth) as his particular form.

Dr. Welldon's desire for a chapel.

In a short time after his appointment, Dr. Welldon began to influence the tone of the School as regards corporal punishment. With some difficulty he introduced the custom of giving impositions in the place of the more forcible and more usual system of frequent appeals to the rod. He then turned his attention to providing for the spiritual wants of the School, and in 1848 made his first proposition to the Governours for the erection of a Chapel. They, however, did not see the necessity for it, more especially as they had no funds at their disposal for the purpose.

The Tercentenary.

On July 26th, 1853, the Tercentenary of the School was celebrated. It was the day of the Annual Visitation, which was commenced by a service at ten o'clock in the morning, with a sermon preached by Dr. Sumner, the Archbishop of Canterbury; there was a larger collection than usual of Old Boys and friends of the School, and Dr. Welldon was presented by the boys with a handsome silver vase, forming a centrepiece for a table, together with a plaster model of the School[1]. In 1858 the increasing want of accommodation caused the erection of the three wooden class-rooms at the side of the playground, which, though small and inconvenient, were all that the funds of the School would allow of the Governours erecting. In fact, in answer to Dr. Welldon's pressing appeal for more room, the Skinners' Company were compelled to answer that through want of funds it was hopeless for them to consider at present the subject of further enlargements. However, the consent of the Governours was obtained the same year by the Doctor to the object he had had at heart for many years—the erection of a School Chapel, for which the Governours gave a site in the School grounds. The only condition attached to the permission was that the School estate should be at no expense in the matter. The funds were provided through the personal exertions of Dr. Welldon, aided by the interest the Old Boys took in the School; and on May 23rd, 1859, the Bishop of Ripon laid the foundation-stone, with this inscription on it:—Hunc lapidem *akrogoniaion* ædis hujus ad majorem Dei gloriam, et in usum Scholæ Tunbridgiensis condendæ Robertus, Episcopus Riponensis, a. d. x cal. Jun., A.D. MDCCCLIX. Patroni, vicini, magistri, alumni pecuniam contulerunt. J. I. Welldon, D.C.L., archididascalo; Wadmore et Baker, architectis; et G. Punnett, fabro. "Nisi Dominus domum ædificaverit, in vanum laboraverunt qui ædificant eam." On October 25th the Archbishop of Canterbury, Dr. Sumner, formally opened it, in the presence of the Visitor, the Warden of All Souls' College, Oxford, the Master and Wardens of the Skinners' Company, and a

---

[1] Vide *Illustrated London News*, Sept. 22, 1866.

considerable number of visitors connected one way or the other with the interests of the School.

Its style. The style of the Chapel is early English decorated; and it is built to hold about 200 people. It is about 75 feet long by 25 feet broad, with an organ-chamber and vestry on the north side. The seats are of coloured pine, and arranged parallel with the north and south sides; the roof is boarded with the same material, and is decorated with six arched ribs of woodwork, by which it is divided into six bays. These ribs spring from elegant shafts of polished Devonshire marble, with carved caps and bosses. The east end is lighted by a handsome window with five lights, and the west end with a pair of two-light windows. The architects were Messrs. Wadmore and Baker, the former a resident in the town and an Old Boy, and to his trouble and interest in the matter the School are much indebted for the elegant simplicity of the design and the careful execution of it. The total cost of its erection and fitting up was about 2500*l*. The design provided for a bell-turret, which has, for want of funds, been omitted. At present efforts are being made to fill the two west windows to the memory of Drs. Vicesimus and Thomas Knox. The old elm-tree, familiar to all Old Boys of more than twelve years' standing, the survivor of a row of elms stretching down to the roadway, was cut down to make room for the Chapel.

Dr. Welldon's suggestions as to the disposal of the money arising from the sale of School property. In 1862 Dr. Welldon, in answer to the Governours' inquiry as to the best disposition of the money realized by the sale of School property to the Midland Railway Company, recommended the erection of a new School-building, and the purchase of the ground of five houses on the south side of the School as likely to be property valuable

THE INTERIOR OF THE CHAPEL, LOOKING EAST

at a future period; three of which houses, together with their sites, were bought by the School in 1866, as well as a strip of land behind the School-house.

The foundation stone of the new buildings was laid on May 9th, 1863, though the actual works had been commenced two months previously. The Master of the Skinners' Company, Mr. George Legg, presided on the occasion, and a considerable number of the Governours attended him. The inscription on the foundation stone runs as follows:— *Foundation stone of the new School laid.*

"Hanc Scholam ab Andrea Judd, milite, fundatam et munifice dotatam, A.D. MDLIII. curatores ejus honorata Pellipariorum Societas de integro struxerunt et ædibus cum amphoribus tum magis hodiernis discipulorum usibus accommodatis ornaverunt. Lapidem auspicalem posuit vii^{mo} idus Maias, A.D. MDCCCLXIII. Georgius Legg, Armiger, hujus Societatis præfectus annuus. *The inscription on it.*

G. Trist,
F. Howell,
S. Wix,
F. Turner,
} Custodibus.

T. G. Kensit, Notario.
J. I. Welldon,
E. I. Welldon,
} Ludimagistris.

E. H. Burnell, Architecto.
G. Punnett, Redemtore.

"Timor Domini principium sapientiæ."
PROV. i. v. 7.

Several newspapers, coins, and photographs of the Masters and boys, were hermetically enclosed in a leaden box, which was placed in the middle of the stone. The final demolition of the old building and the inhabitation of the new took place at the commencement of the Midsummer term, 1864.

The style and description of the new School.

The style of the architecture is early English decorated (in accordance with that of the Chapel), and the material used in the construction of the building is the sandstone found in the neighbouring quarries. The building faces south-east, as the former one did, and stands back from the road about thirty-five yards; it forms, with the Chapel and the Head Master's private house, three sides of a square. The main portion of the building is an oblong, 208 feet long by 34 broad; there are three wings running out at the back; one at the north end, in which are the Lower School class-rooms;

The exterior.

one in the middle, forming the sixth form room, with the library above; and the remaining one at the south end, forming the dining-hall, with the infirmary above. In the middle of the front of the building a tower stands out, rising to the height of 66 feet, with a belfry at the top. There are nine class-rooms, averaging 24 feet by 18 in area, and 12 in height. The great school-room is 75 feet long, 30 broad, and 25 high. Over this is the cubicle room of the same size, except that it has a slanting roof. These

The interior.

cubicles are 34 in number; each of them is 12 feet long, and 6 feet 6 inches broad, with partitions running to the height of 6 feet. This room is very light, cheerful, and airy, and without exaggeration may be said to afford as good and as healthy accommodation as any school, public or private, can give. Opposite the front entrance of the School is the sixth form room, with the School library above, each 20 feet long, 16 broad, and 12 high. The sixth form class-room is over the entrance-hall, and has a bay window looking out towards the high road. To the left of the front

entrance are class-rooms, a washing-room, and a large corridor leading to the school-house dining-hall, a lofty room 25 feet high, 40 long, and 25 broad, with a gallery running along one end of it. On the first floor is a corridor over the one on the ground floor, and two class-rooms of the same size as those below, and two smaller rooms for the use of the two school-house Assistant Masters. Parallel with the cubicle room, and over the class-rooms on the first-floor, are dormitories for the smaller boys, bath-rooms, and the House-Master's bedrooms; and over the dining-hall, at the south end of the building, is the infirmary, consisting of three large and airy rooms and bath-rooms, which can be completely shut off from the rest of the house, in case there should be any necessity. *The interior.*

The cricket pavilion deserves mention here, for its neatness of style, beauty of situation, and general usefulness to the School. It was built of ornamental brickwork in 1860, under the gratuitous superintendence of Mr. Wadmore, and has a pretty exterior, together with a very well arranged interior. It consists of a dining-hall 35 feet by 20 feet, two smaller rooms 15 feet by 10 feet each, a verandah, and a covered balcony for the scorers; and the total cost of its erection, defrayed by subscriptions from the Governours, the Master, and Old and Present Tonbridgians, aided by those then at the School, amounted to 370*l*. *The cricket pavilion.*

Subjoined is a list of the Head Boys at Skinners' Day in each year, since 1844:— *List of Head Boys.*

   1844. P. R. Sandilands.
   1845. G. F. L. Bampfield.
   1846. G. F. Wilgress.
   1847. J. Stroud.
   1848. A. H. Hore.

1849, 1850, 1851. M. Melville.
1852. A. P. Howell.
1853. W. R. Morfill.
1854. P. G. Skipworth.
1855. B. H. Alford.
1856. J. T. Howard.
1857. R. A. Pryor.
1858. H. St. J. Reade.
1859. R. H. Burrows.
1860. J. Greathead.
1861. A. Simpson.
1862. T. F. Burra.
1863. W. S. R. Greenhill.
1864, 1865. H. A. Richardson.
1866. W. B. Lindsell.
1867. A. W. D. Campbell.
1868, 1869. F. W. Hughes-Hughes.

The Scholars from Tonbridge School are eligible to the following Fellowships and Exhibitions.

Scholarships and Exhibitions belonging to the School.

A Scholarship, worth 100*l.* a year, at St. John's College, Oxford, founded by Sir Thomas Whyte.

Sixteen Exhibitions of 100*l.* per annum each, tenable at any college of either University, and payable out of the Founder's endowment.

Six Exhibitions of 13*l.* per annum each, tenable at any college of either University, founded by Sir Thomas Smith.

One Scholarship at Brazenose College, Oxford, of 17*l.* 9*s.* 6*d.* per annum, founded by Mr. Henry Fisher.

One Exhibition of 2*l.* 13*s.* 4*d.* per annum, founded by Mr. Thomas Lampard.

One Exhibition of 4*l*. per annum (in default of scholars from Sevenoaks School), founded by Mr. Robert Holmedon.

Two Exhibitions of 75*l*. per annum each, tenable at Jesus College, Cambridge (in default of scholars from Sevenoaks School), founded by Lady Mary Boswell.

Two Exhibitions of 6*l*. per annum each, founded by Mr. Worrall.

Two Exhibitions of 50*l*. are annually given by the Head and Second Masters for boys under fourteen years of age, each tenable for two years, after which time they are thrown open to all the School.

The following School List of July 22, 1844, is the earliest complete list of the School obtainable; and on that account is, perhaps, of some interest:— *School List in 1844.*

Examiner.

Rev. S. WALDEGRAVE, Fellow of All Souls', Oxford.

Masters.

Rev. J. I. WELLDON, M.A., Head Master.
Rev. T. BROWN, Second Master.

Assistant Masters.

ARTHUR WOLFE, Esq., B.A., Fellow of Clare Hall, Cambridge.
EDWARD IND WELLDON, Esq., B.A., Scholar of Queens' College, Cambridge.

Orat. Congrat.
Sandilands 1mus.

VI.

Sandilands 1mus.
Willis 1mus.
Bampfield.
Gatliff 1mus.
Brown 1mus.
Wilgress.

Gatliff 2dus.
Buttanshaw.
Stroud 1mus.

V. 1.

Miller.
Pearson.
Sandilands 3tius.

May 1mus.
Hore.

2.

Wilkinson 1mus.
Burra 1mus.
Harward.
Acworth.
Sandilands 2dus.
Haycock.
Bailey.
Springett.
Witherby.
Hare 1mus.

3.

Jordan.
Wilson.
Brown 2dus.
Cobb 1mus.
Bowman 1mus.
Dury.

IV. 1.

Waddilove 1mus.
Bridgett 1mus.
Larking 1mus.
Martin.
Burra 2dus.
Walford.
Gattliff 3tius.
Ellis.
Smith 1mus.
Hare 2dus.

2.

May 2dus.
Harwood.

Seddon.
Hammond.
Puckle 2dus.
Morgan.
Vaughan.
Puckle 1mus.
Fonblanque.
Nicholas.

3.

Banks.
Kier.
Swansborough.
Isaacson.
Wyatt.

III. 1.

Canham.
Bell.
Barnett.
Rolfe 1mus.
Brown 3tius.
Wormald 1mus.
Beeching 1mus.
Stroud 2dus.
Cobb 2dus.
Willis 2dus.
Elers 1mus.
Sprye 1mus.

2.

Bridgett 2dus.
Magnay.
Bowman 2dus.
Elster.
Chippindale.
Hare 3tius.
Hardinge 1mus.

3.

Sprye 2dus.
Smith 2dus.
Davey.
Wormald 2dus.
Waddilove 2dus.
Bull.
Lake.
Puckle 3tius.
Hardinge 2dus.
Scoones.

II.

Bigsby.
Cobham.
Wormald 3tius.
Arnold.
Rolfe 2dus.
Stroud 3tius.

Brown 4tus.
Hardinge 3tius.
Smyly.
Elers 2dus.
Monypeny.
Wilkinson 2dus.

I.

Stedman.
Beeching 2dus.
Larkin 2dus.
Beeching 3tius.
West.
Cousins.
Beecham.

Cargill.
Bowman 3tius.
Turner.
Humphrey.

The Prize for Greek Verse ⎫ was adjudged to Willis 1mus.
,,   Latin Verse ⎭
,,   Latin Prose   ,,   Sandilands 1mus.
,,   Mathematics   ,,   Buttanshaw.
,,   French   ,,   Bridgett 1mus.

The Bonfire was an old institution, intermitted from 1832 to 1841 in consequence of a serious accident with fireworks. In the latter year Tamplin, the head boy then, induced Dr. Knox to permit the revival of it on condition that there were to be no fireworks, and for some little time after that there were none. For a fortnight or more before the 5th of November the Bonfire was the great subject of interest. To meet the expenses of it a subscription was levied throughout the School, the amount being recoverable in the case of defaulters, especially among the Lower

The Bonfire.

The Bonfire.

School, by the summary process of administering "dabs," generally performed by the sharp application of a stick or fives-bat to the open palm of the hand. The subscription was increased by liberal donations from the Masters, the Vicar, and the chief inhabitants of the town, and used to amount to ten or twelve pounds, if not more. The preparations for the fire were made at the lower end of the playground, near where the present fives-court stands. A tall pole, about thirty-five feet high, was driven into the ground, and surrounded with tar barrels in a circle, so as to form a sort of chimney in the centre, in which the air circulated and drew up the flames. These barrels were in their turn surrounded by a thick coating of hop-bines; and the whole formed a conical-shaped pile rising to the height of thirty feet, and covering a circle of about seventy yards in circumference. The making up of the Guy Fawkes was entrusted to Killick, the School porter; and at eight o'clock in the evening it was placed in the front hall of the School, to be inspected by the ladies and visitors who were invited in considerable numbers to see the fire from a safe position at the windows at the back of the School. Guy Fawkes was then carried down the playground, and hoisted to the top of the pole in the centre of the bonfire, which Killick lighted by creeping in through a hole left for the purpose. The townspeople used to fill the School grounds to see the sight; and altogether the scene was one not easily to be forgotten. When fairly alight the heat was intense, and the reflection cast a red glare upon the old Church and Castle. Fireworks were sometimes let off by the boys; and at the conclusion, between ten and eleven o'clock, water was poured over the burning mass, but the embers smouldered on for several days, which boys, with a turn for cooking, made use of to roast potatoes, &c., obtained sometimes from the town, sometimes, it was hinted (though, of course, without foundation), from the garden of the Second Master. The Bonfire was discontinued in 1858, in consequence of the effect of an accident to one of the boys.

The present BISHOP OF DERRY was educated under Dr. Knox between 1836 and 1840, and afterwards went to Winchester. From there he went to Oxford and entered at Brazenose, where he graduated "Honorary Fourth" in classics in 1847. He obtained the Denyer Theological prize in 1850. In 1857 he won the University prize by his poem "The Waters of Babylon," and in 1867 he ran his competitors close for the chair of poetry at Oxford.

<small>The Bishop of Derry.</small>

He is the eldest son of the Rev. Robert Alexander, who held the Rectory and Prebend of Aghadoey, near Coleraine, in the Diocese, and twenty-one years ago he himself began his ministry in what will now be his own cathedral, having been ordained in 1847. Since then he has held in the Diocese the three successive rectories of Termonamongel, with a population of about 1400 ; Fahen, which he held for five years ; and Strabane (or Camus-juxta-Mourne), with a population of 1000, which he has held for the last seven years.

In 1853 he was selected to write and recite the inaugural ode at the installation of the Earl of Derby as Chancellor of the University of Oxford.

As a prose writer Dr. Alexander has contributed a great number of valuable papers to many of our first serials. Those upon the Incarnation and Resurrection of our Lord in the last two numbers of *Good Words*, and upon the

Confessions of St. Augustine in the *Contemporary Review*, have attracted considerable attention. He is also one of those chosen to write "The Speaker's Commentary," his part being the Epistle of St. John. Only three Irish Clergymen have been associated in this work. From the period of his ordination he has been invariably connected with large and important parishes, and he is more likely to get on smoothly among the Ulster folk than one not conversant with the north.

Dr. Alexander was in 1864 promoted to the Deanery of Emly, and in 1867 was made Bishop of the Diocese over which he now presides. His wife is the authoress of the well-known "Hymns for Little Children."

The Commissioners' Report on the School. The following extracts from the recent Report issued by the Endowed Schools' Commission gives a full account of the present position and state of the School[1]:—

This School was founded by Sir Andrew Judde, Alderman of London, in the reigns of Edward VI. and Queen Elizabeth. He reserved the usual power of administration to himself during his life, and after his death bequeathed the government to the Skinners' Company, to be exercised with the advice of All Souls' College, Oxford.

This bequest was attempted to be set aside, but it was eventually and fully confirmed by two Statutes of the 14th and 31st years of Queen Elizabeth.

The School continued on this footing up to the date of the Report of the Charity Commission (1819); but a suit in Chancery having been instituted respecting the School estates, and the application of them, a decree was made in

---

[1] Report of Commission, vol. i. p. 525.

1802, directing an inquiry before a Master of the Court with a view to the enlargement of the Scheme; and upon his report two orders have been made by the Court in 1825 and 1844, containing a full Scheme accordingly, which the Governors have published under the title of Statutes and Regulations, and of which we have received a copy. Under this scheme the School is now governed. We have not been furnished with any copies of the early documents of this foundation, but the first twenty clauses of the Scheme (thirty-four in all) would appear from internal evidence to be substantially from the Founder's hands. The Commissioners mention an instrument called the Statute of the School of Tonbridge, of the 6th of Elizabeth, conveying part of Sir A. Judde's intentions, and in which three points may be noted:— *The Scheme of 1825 and additions of 1844.*

1st. That boarders are distinctly recognized.

2nd. That a somewhat stringent entrance examination, including perfect reading of Latin as well as English, and writing, is provided, and

3rd. That (apparently) a boy was to be dismissed if after five years he had not "learnt his grammar."

The Letters Patent contained a provision similar to that in those for the foundation of the Birmingham School, that the whole property of the endowment should be applied solely to the payment of two Masters, and to repairs. In neither case does this provision appear to have been adhered to. *Application of endowment.*

The Skinners' Company assert a claim similar to that of the Mercers' Company in the case of St. Paul's School, to the absolute ownership of the proceeds of the property, after making certain payments out of it. The payments appear to have included the maintenance of the School, at least on a certain scale and within the limits of the original area, the town and parish of Tonbridge. The Commissioners, however, doubted if the claim could be maintained, and suggested that it should be solved by a judicial decision. A suit, as stated above, was acordingly instituted, and it was decided in 1821 (and the decision confirmed on appeal) that the School was entitled to the most valuable part of the property disposed of by Sir A. Judde, viz. the estates situated in St. Pancras and in All Hallows, the annual rental of which at that date was 3190*l*., and to an insignificant contribution out of the remaining estates towards the expenses of the Skinners' visitation, and of repairing the old school-house. The new Scheme enlarged the area for Foundationers as aforesaid, established a second class of boys as distinct from the Foundationers, namely, boys from any part of the United Kingdom, at a considerably higher rate of payment (no part of the education being absolutely gratuitous to any boys, except Latin and Greek, according to the rule often in force in ancient Grammar Schools); defined the number of boarders, the number and value of the Exhibitions, the position and emoluments of the Masters, the Examinations, and other details. But it has not essentially varied the character of the School, as it has been from its foundation. It is essentially a Classical School, or, as we should say, a School of the first grade, and in its predominant character it is a Boarding School. The Company, with the advice of All Souls', have the general power of government and regulation, but the Head Master, subject to such power, has the entire charge of the studies and discipline of the boys.

Provisions of present Scheme.

The Governors state that no material increase of the revenues is in early prospect. Mr. Elton, however, says that in about three years probably there will be an increase of perhaps 2000*l.* a year, and another somewhat later. But the great increase above alluded to will not be till 1906. *The School income.*

The net School income is stated on an average of five years at 2643*l.* Great additions are to be made to this in respect of payments for board and for various *extras;* but on the whole we do not think that the present amount of endowment is such as to warrant us, considering the work actually done by the School, in advising any essential change in its objects.

The boys, especially the boarders, are manifestly for the most part sons of gentry; though a small number only go direct to the Universities, many go into the army and civil service; a very fair proportion of them are above the age of sixteen, which is an admitted test of the character of a school, and the School is of well-established repute among the higher Schools of the country.

The amount of payment, especially for day-boys, is a fair question for consideration. But Mr. Elton does not suggest material reduction till the revenues are increased; and considering the social position of the boarders, it seems to us that their payments are moderate, and that they do substantially benefit by the existence of the endowment. The highest bill was 128*l.*, the lowest 70*l.*, the average 95*l.*

The instruction given in the School is in the main uniform, and there does not appear to be a Modern Department in it. Mr. Elton says there was "a modern form," and that it was dropped from want of space, and from *Character of instruction.*

the fees being too high. The Head Master alludes probably to this when he says there were Physical Science Classes, which have been discontinued.

It is a question whether Mr. Elton is right in advising the creation of a Modern Department, wholly separate from the Classical; but it seems clear that to some extent the balance inclines too much in favour of classics, and, though cautiously and probably only with changes in detail, it should be redressed. Mr. Elton says that non-classical subjects are "neglected in the higher forms;" and the Head Master himself states expressly that "little encouragement is given to *mathematics and other studies.*"

We do not think it necessary to go into detail on this subject. Valuable suggestions will be found upon it in the brief Report of Mr. Elton; nor can it be supposed that the Governors would find any difficulty in dealing with the matter, with such aid as they would receive from a man of the ability and experience of Dr. Welldon, the Head Master.

Local privileges. There is, then, the usual question of local privileges for foundationers. The area for the enjoyment of those privileges is measured by a radius of ten miles from Tonbridge Church. This is large compared with such a case as Bedford; and perhaps, considering the rural character of the district, no relaxation as to day-boys would have any great practical effect; but as to boarders it would be material.

Again, though there is no exclusion of an absolute character, as at Bedford, of non-foundationers from Exhibitions and Prizes, there is a very invidious and objectionable distinction made to their prejudice. No non-foundationer can enjoy any of the valuable Exhibitions of the School, if a foundationer on examination can be found "duly qualified."

Mr. Elton states, and it is obviously inevitable, that so indeterminate a ground of preference has led to constant disputes; and the parents of foundationers have contended, not unreasonably it would seem, that their boys have a right to election, as against others, if they have the bare *minimum* of attainment that would enable the holder to pass through the Universities.

We think this distinction should be abolished: and we venture to recommend, following our general rule, that the foundationers should be chosen by competition, and that the foundation should eventually (with due consideration for the vested interests of present residents) be open to all England, as much as those of Eton and Winchester.

We should add, that Mr. Elton says of the whole School that the teaching is "very good of its kind," and speaks with unqualified and hearty approval and admiration of its discipline, comfort, and general arrangements.

As soon as the increase of 2000*l*. a year, which Mr. Elton thinks that there is reason to expect, shall accrue, we are of opinion that the claims of the neighbourhood to good second grade and third grade schools should be considered. Such schools should probably be day schools. But their precise character and situation ought to be left to be determined by the Governors. *Second and third grade Schools to be added hereafter.*

The Governing Body should, in our opinion, be remodelled in accordance with our general recommendations. The Skinners' Company should name one half, the other half should be named by the Provincial Board, which we shall hereafter describe. *Governing Body.*

REPORT BY C. J. ELTON, ESQ.

This School is already of considerable importance, and its revenues will within forty years be increased so largely that it is necessary to consider with much minuteness the merits of the Scheme by which it is governed.

The revenues. In three years the revenues will very probably be increased by 1800*l.* or 2000*l.* yearly; after a further augmentation a few years later, they will become very great in 1906, when an important building lease of land in London will fall in. The probable revenue has been variously estimated at 80,000*l.* per annum (by Mr. Gladstone, when Chancellor of the Exchequer), and at 20,000*l.* per annum by the School authorities. It will probably much exceed the latter estimate. The Founder's intentions were:—(1) To provide free instruction in grammar to the boys residing in Tonbridge and "the adjacent country;" and (2) To benefit the town by bringing boarders to the houses of the Head Master and of the inhabitants.

The Founder's intentions. The School having become rich by accident, as it may be said, the Founder's intentions have been disregarded in most points. The instruction is comparatively expensive, and it is not considered desirable that townspeople, not being Masters in the School, should receive boarders. In one matter, however, his (supposed) intention is followed in a manner which threatens to destroy the usefulness of his School. In the Schemes of 1825 and 1844 the words "adjacent country" have been construed to mean a district measured along the roads by a radius of ten miles from Tonbridge Church. All boys whose parents have *bonâ fide* resided within this district for five years are on the foundation; all others are in "the second class." Boys of both classes are eligible to the sixteen Founder's Exhibitions, each worth 100*l.* per annum, for which a yearly competitive examination is held; *but foundationers, if duly qualified, are to be preferred to all others.* No one knows what is the due qualification; the parents contend, with some reason, that every foundationer must be preferred, if there is a reasonable hope that he will pass through Oxford or Cambridge. Foundationers' privileges.

Great disputes have arisen on this matter between such parents and the Masters and Examiners of the School, and legal proceedings have more than once been threatened. It is found that when the number of foundationers in the fifth and sixth forms is small, idleness is encouraged by this rule, and deserving boys of the second class are disheartened. It is not known that the Founder intended any such distinction of classes, nor, if he did so intend, is there any reason for retaining the present system. The parents of the foundationers are not the tradesmen of Tonbridge, but for the most part persons of a somewhat higher social position, living in the place in order to gain the local privilege above-mentioned for their sons. It may fairly be doubted whether the privilege was created in 1825 for their benefit. The Governors (the Skinners' Company), the Head and Assistant Masters, and the Examiners appointed from time to time by All Souls' College and the Skinners' Company, are all sensible of the evils now produced by it, and wish that the scheme may be improved.

Four classical Exhibitions of great value are too much for the School in its present condition. Two at least of them should be given for proficiency in mathematics and modern The Exhibitions languages. At present a small number of boys (about three per cent.) go to the Universities, and fewer still would go if these classical prizes were diminished in number. At present the gain of an Exhibition is often a loss to the boy.

The Exhibitions should be thrown open to competition, increased in number, reduced in value, and apportioned between a classical and a modern department. More minor Exhibitions tenable at the School should be provided. An attempt lately made to get these small Exhibitions established by the Governors has failed since the date of my visit.

<small>Character of instruction and suggestions for its alteration.</small> Taking into account the professions which are usually chosen by the boys on leaving School, it seems very necessary that a modern department should in some way be created. A "modern form" existed for a short time; but the fees were too high for its success, and separate rooms with separate Masters were required. Latin should still be taught to all the boys, but modern languages might replace classical composition and the study of Greek for boys on the modern side of the School. At present the teaching is mainly classical, with a fair amount of instruction in French, mathematics, and some other "extra subjects." The classical teaching is good. The sixth form is well advanced, and the scholars examined by me did very well in Thucydides and Juvenal, and passed a good examination in ancient history. One of the Exhibitioners was well informed in modern history, but I should not think that sufficient importance was attached to this subject. The younger classes did well. Their construing of easy authors was accurate, and their knowledge of Latin and Greek grammar was satisfactory. I was much pleased with the mathematical papers sent up by some of the higher boys during my

visit, but there is a tendency in the two highest forms to neglect mathematics and modern languages, the whole tendency of the School being classical. Much more attention should be paid to modern subjects. I cannot speak too highly of the care taken by the Head Master to maintain the discipline and promote the comfort of the whole School. There is a fine Chapel and a good playground, and the arrangements for boarders in the School-house are excellent.

Considering the approaching increase of the revenues of this charity, I think that the following alterations should be made, in addition to those above proposed :— *Suggestions for the future government of the School.*

When the income expands, the fees for tuition should be considerably reduced. The necessity for paying private tutors should be removed. No charge should be made for French or mathematics. The modern department should be entirely separated from the classical School. The salaries of the Masters should be raised, and not, as now, paid chiefly by the Head and Second Masters. Two public Examiners at least should be annually appointed. If possible, public Examiners in the modern languages should be provided annually. The Second Master should be responsible to the Head Master, and not, as now, to the Governors alone. When the course of instruction is somewhat changed, and local privileges abolished, the School will rise prominently into notice.

The tradesmen of Tonbridge are not, on the whole, satisfied with the state of the School. It is true that the large number of the boarders in the school-house and other houses gives a great stimulus to trade. Again, many people are attracted, by the comparative cheapness of the education for day-boys, to live at Tonbridge for the three years necessary to gain the full privileges of the foundation. But they cannot send their sons to the School for two reasons: the education is so thoroughly classical, and they fear class prejudices among the boys. There is one tradesman's son from the town now in the School. No such feeling has ever been displayed towards him, but the suspicion of such an evil as social pride among the present set of boys is in itself a great misfortune. There is not, after all, such a great separation of ranks as has been imagined. If the School were thrown more open to the tradesmen of the town, it is absurd to suppose that the present set of boys would be injured by their society. It is not anticipated that the very poor tradesmen would in any case use the foundation, although without doubt the clever son of the poorest man should have a chance of entering the town School by means of an Exhibition, or after an Examination. If modern classes were fairly established, I think that a good many of the wealthier shopkeepers would use the School for their children, and it is possible that the fear of such a result has hitherto impeded the free development of this modern department. It is not unlikely that many of these boys would choose to go to the University if successful in gaining a good Exhibition. At present the system of education is that of a large public school sending a majority of its scholars to the University, but the results are disproportionate to the means employed, as has been shown above. Few go to Oxford and Cambridge, and of those few some had better remain away. A young man without money, and destined for one of the minor professions, cannot properly afford to spend three years in taking a bare degree or

The position of the tradesmen of the town as regards the School.

small honours, even though he has taken a rich Exhibition from the School. All the scholars, after reaching the middle of the School, should have an option of preparing specially for their various professions, with a chance of help from Exhibitions.

It would no doubt be a good thing for the town if a Middle School could be established in connexion with the Grammar School, which would supply the latter with a succession of industrious boys promoted by merit shown in the Annual Examinations. The funds of the charity will be quite sufficient in a few years to do this. *The establishment of a Middle School.*

It may be observed that the School was intended to benefit the poorer inhabitants of the town. This may be collected from the facts that the endowment was originally of very trifling value, and that the Statutes, as approved by Archbishop Parker, provided for the gratuitous instruction of such day-boys as could write competently and read English and Latin perfectly. *Original object of the School.*

In 1765 the Skinners' Company took counsel with the most eminent lawyers as to the extent of the freedom of the School, and resolved "that the children of the town and parish of Tonbridge, qualified as above described, should be instructed without payment of any consideration except the statutable entrance fee. The Exhibitions also were defined to be for the benefit of 'poor scholars.'"

A sum of money was bequeathed by a Mr. Strong in the last century "for the apprenticing to some marine business of a scholar educated at the great School in Tonbridge." The Head Master is desirous of claiming the income of this fund as an Exhibition for a boy from his School meant for the naval service, civil engineering, ship-building, or the *Strong's legacy.*

like. The inhabitants of the town are, however, opposed to this plan, asserting, with some reason, that too much of the benefit of the charity has already been diverted from the tradesmen and poorer residents in Tonbridge.

QUESTIONS

ADDRESSED TO THE TRUSTEES OF ENDOWED SCHOOLS FOR BOYS COMPRISED IN THE COMMISSION; WITH THEIR ANSWERS[1].

A.

CONSTITUTION AND ENDOWMENT.

Constitution and Endowment.

1. By what name is the School commonly known?—The Free Grammar School of Sir Andrew Judd, Knight, commonly called Tonbridge Free Grammar School.

2. When, and by whom, and by what instrument was it founded?—Founded by Sir Andrew Judd, Knight, by Charter of Edward VI., A.D. 1553.

3. In what town, if any, and in what parish is it situate?—In the town and parish of Tonbridge.

4. What is the number of the population of such town and parish?—7147 in the town, and 20,001 in the parish.

5. Does any large proportion of the neighbouring population belong to the farming, manufacturing, mining, seafaring, or to any other, and what class?—The largest proportion is the farming class.

6. Is the School (*a*) a separate foundation, or (*b*) a branch of any foundation, comprising also other and what objects?—Separate foundation.

7. In the latter case—(*a*) are the endowments of the School separate, or (*b*) is it entitled to any, and what, share of the income of the whole establishment?

8. Is any special power in force for the modification of the

---

[1] Commissioners' Report, vol. iii. p. 423.

Statutes or constitution of the charity? and in whom is it vested?—Yes; vested in the Governors of the School.

9. Has any such modification been made, whether under such special power, or under any, and what, general jurisdiction?—Yes.

10. If any new scheme has been established for the government of the School within the last fifty years, please to send a copy of such scheme.—A new scheme for the future establishment of the School was made in the year 1825 under the order of the Court of Chancery. A copy is sent.

11. Mention any parts of the Statutes or Ordinances which, without being formally repealed, have been dispensed with, or ceased to be observed.—None.

12. Will you add any reasons which appear to you to justify any such non-observance?

13. Where are the instrument of foundation, and any subsequent or separate Statutes or Ordinances governing the School, and its other muniments, deposited?—The Charter is a document on record, and the present scheme is on the Records of the Court of Chancery.

14. Are they, or copies of them, accessible to the public?—Yes.

15. Are the School site and buildings well adapted to their purpose?—Yes; they have been recently rebuilt.

16. By whom is the School property actually managed?—By the Governors and Trustees, the Skinners' Company.

17. State the average gross income derived from the whole endowments during the last five years.—3613$l.$ 12$s.$ 5$d.$, average gross annual income.

18. State the average net amount of such income applicable to the purposes of the foundation during the same years, after the allowance of all outgoings payable in respect of the properties, the expenses of management, and other deductions.—2643$l.$ 6$s.$ 11$d.$, average net annual income after all outgoings.

19. State what portion of that amount has been applied to the purposes of the School during the same years.—The whole.

20. Please to send a balance-sheet of all receipts and expenditure on account of the endowments during the last year, stating any arrears of income received, and any income accrued due but not received at the close of the year.

21. Are the accounts of the School property regularly audited? and at what period? and by whom?—The accounts are audited by a committee of Governors at four quarterly periods of the year.

22. If in any year the income exceeds the expenditure, who holds the balance, and what is done with it?—The income seldom exceeds the expenditure, but if such be the case the balance is carried over to the requirements of the following year.

23. If in any year the expenditure exceeds the income, how is the deficiency met?—The amount has then been advanced by the Governors.

24. Is any material increase or diminution of income to be expected at any early period, on the expiration of existing leases, or under any new dispositions of the property, or otherwise?—There is no early expectation of any material increase or diminution.

25. Are there any, and what, ecclesiastical benefices comprised in the endowments?—No.

26. In whose patronage are any such benefices?

27. By whom is each held?

28. Has the incumbent of any such benefice any, and what, present or past relation to the School in respect of any office discharged by him, or otherwise?

29. Are there any exhibitions or scholarships at any University appropriated to the School separately, or with other schools, by the original or any later endowments? If so, state (*a*) the total number; (*b*) the amount of each; (*c*) the period for which it is tenable; (*d*) the conditions of tenure.—Yes. Sixteen exhibitions of 100*l*. per annum each, tenable for four years at either University. Six of 16*l*., tenable for seven years. One of 20*l*. per annum, confined to Brasenose College. One of 2*l*. 13*s*. 4*d*. in the election of the vicar and churchwardens of Tonbridge. One of 40*l*. per annum on default of scholars from the School at Seven Oaks. Two of 50*l*. per annum to Jesus College, Cambridge, in default of scholars from Seven Oaks School [1].

30. Are there any exhibitions tenable at the School? If so, give the same particulars.—No.

---

[1] Vide p. 30.

GOVERNMENT OF SCHOOL.

31. State the names, descriptions, and residences of the Trustees or Governing Body of the School property.—The Master and Wardens and Court of Assistants of the Skinners' Company, Skinners' Hall, Dowgate Hill.

32. Are there any *ex officio* Trustees or Governors? and if so, to what offices or positions is the trust annexed?—No.

33. State what are the means for the renewal or continuance of the trust or management upon the occurrence of any vacancy among the non-official Trustees or Governors.—The Skinners' Company are incorporated by charter, and a perpetual body.

34. Are there any particular qualifications, whether of name, kin, birth, residence, place of education, religious creed, profession, employment, or other, required in Trustees or Governors?—No.

35. Do the Governors actually exercise any control over—(*a*) the internal management and regulations of the School; (*b*) the appointment or dismissal of the Master, or any of the Masters, whether on the foundation or not; (*c*) the admission or expulsion of the boys; (*d*) the studies; (*e*) the discipline; (*f*) the payments by the boys; (*g*) the conduct of examinations and appointment of examiners?—Yes; in such respect as is prescribed by the Statutes.

36. Is the consent of the Bishop of the diocese or other person required and actually obtained by the Governors for exercising any of their powers?—No.

OBJECTS OF TRUST.

37. For whose benefit was the School founded, as set forth in the Deed of Foundation?—See preamble to the Statutes.

38. Is the endowment (*a*) for the education of boys only; or (*b*) in whole or in part applicable to the education of girls?—Boys only.

39. Are there any, and what, particular qualifications, absolute or preferential, whether of name, kin, birth, residence, age, religious creed, profession or occupation of parents, poverty, or other circumstances required in candidates for admission to the School, or to any advantage thereof?—No.

40. Has any class of boys a right to claim admission to the

advantages of the Foundation?—Yes; such whose parents reside in Kent within a radius of ten miles of Tonbridge Church.

41. Can boys of that class, if any, be rejected for incompetence or any other reason?—Yes; if under eight years of age, or unable to write competently and read English perfectly.

42. Can they be dismissed or expelled?—Yes; as regulated by the Statutes.

43. What does the Foundation require to be taught in the School?—Latin and Greek.

44. Does the Foundation provide any other benefits for the scholars than instruction; as clothing, board, advancement in life, or the like? If so, specify them.—No.

45. Are the benefits of the Foundation, whether instruction or other, open to all the scholars?—Yes; but limited as before mentioned in answer to Question 40.

46. If there is any limitation, are the recipients selected by merit or nominated, or do they succeed by seniority, or in virtue of any other and what qualifications?—Only such qualifications as mentioned in answer to Question 41.

47. Is the number of boys entitled to the benefits of the Foundation increasing or diminishing?—Increasing.

Masters (including Usher) of School.

Masters (including Usher) of School.

48. What is the title and description of the Head and other Foundation Masters?—The Head Master. The Usher.

49. How many Foundation Masters are there?—Two, as above.

50. By whom are the Head and other Foundation Masters appointed?—The Head Master is appointed by the Governors. The Usher is appointed by the Head Master.

51. Is the right of appointing the Master alienable?—No.

52. Are any, and what, qualifications, absolute or preferential, whether of school, university, religious creed, profession, age, or other circumstances, ordered to be required in the Head or other Masters?—The Head Master is required by the Statutes to be a well-reported Master of Arts.

53. Have any such qualifications been in fact required?—Yes; always.

54. Is the office of Master held or tenable with any ecclesiastical or other preferment or office?—The office of Master is not now held with any other preferment, but there is nothing to prevent his doing so.

55. What has been or is the usual practice observed in making the appointment of any Master?—By election of the Governors from candidates.

56. Is the notice of vacancy published, and in what way?—Yes; in the newspapers.

57. Do the present Master or Masters hold office subject to any future alterations as to duties or emoluments?—No.

58. Are any residences provided for the Head or other Foundation Masters?—Yes.

59. If so, are they adapted for the reception of boarders?—Yes.

60. Do the Masters reside in their official residences?—Yes.

61. Are the Masters permitted to receive boarders? with what limitation?—Yes. The Head Master is limited to the number of sixty boarders; the Usher to the number of forty.

62. Does the Head or any other Master make payments to other Masters, or for any other purposes, out of their official receipts?—Yes. The Head Master pays for such extra Masters as are not provided for by the Statutes.

63. What is the average net yearly income of each Master—(*a*) from the endowment; (*b*) from fees for instruction; (*c*) from profits of boarders; (*d*) from any other sources?—The Head Master's salary is 510*l*.; his capitation fees average 560*l*. per annum. The Usher's salary is 205*l*.; his capitation fees average 220*l*. per annum. The profits for boarders average about 1000*l*. for the Head Master. The profits of the Usher for boarders average about 600*l*.

64. Is there any rule or usage respecting superannuation, or any provision for it?—None except the Sixth Article of the Statutes.

65. Does the power of appointing and dismissing Assistant Masters or Teachers, regular or occasional, rest with the Governors or Head Master, or with whom?—Yes; with the Head Master

BALANCE SHEET.

Balance Sheet.— The Skinners' Company in account with the Tonbridge School Estate.

THE SKINNERS' COMPANY IN ACCOUNT WITH THE TONBRIDGE SCHOOL ESTATE, ONE YEAR TO JUNE 23RD, 1864.

Dr.

		£	s.	d.
1863.	To balance of cash brought forward from June 23rd, 1863	74	4	9
1864.	To cash received during the year on account of rents and arrears	3932	4	7
		£4006	9	4

1864.		£	s.	d.
June 26th.	To balance of cash	1290	0	0
	Arrears of rent due at Lady Day . .	560	16	0

Cr.

		£	s.	d.
1863–64.	By cash paid during the year for the various purposes of the School . .	2716	8	1
June 23rd.	By balance of cash carried forward .	1290	1	3
		£4006	9	4

We, being Governors or Trustees of the above-named School, hereby certify that the foregoing statements are correct.

(Signed)   T. G. KENSIT,
Clerk of the Skinners' Company,
Governors of Tonbridge School.

June 12th, 1865.

B.

Character of School.

2. Is the School intended for, and actually used by, boarders or day-boys, or both?—Used by both, and intended for both, Statute 6 (original); Statute 22 (later).

3. If any great change has occurred in the number or character of the surrounding population, state whether, and when, and how, it has (a) affected the success or usefulness of the School; (b) altered the class or habits of the boys attending it.—Many gentry have resorted to Tonbridge Wells and the neighbourhood. The town of Tonbridge has increased in size and in population, but I cannot see that the character of the population is changed. The neighbourhood is agricultural, no great trade has been developed. I am not aware that the School has been affected by these circumstances.

4. From what distance do the day-boys come?—At present only from the town; formerly one or two came from Southborough, three miles distant.

5. Do they (a) remain for the whole day? and if so, where do they dine? or (b) return to their homes between the school hours?—Such boys as have come from Southborough breakfasted and dined with one of the Masters, all others return to their homes between School hours.

6. Can you state generally the profession or occupation of the parents or next friends of the boys, whether day boys or boarders, attending the School?— Generally professional, clergy, officers, lawyers, physicians, surgeons, &c., and their widows.

7. On the average of the last five years, how many boys have within one year of leaving the School gone (a) to any University? (b) to any other place of education?—From 20 to 25 have gone direct to the University, about the same number have gone to military establishments, &c., to be prepared for the army and civil services.

Boarding-Houses.

8. What, if any, authority is necessary to enable any person to keep a boarding-house in connexion with the School?—Being a

Master is sufficient authority, Statute 46. Other housekeepers of Tonbridge may take boarders, having obtained a written licence from the Governors, with testimonial from Head Master, Statute 26.

9. Does the Head Master keep a boarding-house?—Yes.

10. Do any, and what, other Masters keep boarding-houses?—The Second Master, and Senior Assistant Master, and Writing Master at present.

11. Are any boarding-houses kept by other than Masters in the School?—None.

12. Are the boarding-houses generally under the Head Master's control? and does it rest with him, or with what authority, to establish regulations for their management?—Yes.

13. How many meals a day are given to the boarders?—Three to all, breakfast, dinner, and tea. Supper is given to the Upper School boys, and to a few others.

14. Of what does each meal consist?—Breakfast, of tea and bread and butter. Dinner, of beef, mutton, veal, pork rarely, puddings, pies, vegetables of all sorts, and bread and ale. Tea, of tea and bread and butter. Supper, of bread and cheese and ale.

15. What is the largest and what is the smallest number of boys in any one bed-room?—Head Master's house, largest four, smallest one, cubical system. Second Master's house, largest ten, smallest one. Other Masters' vary from four to one.

16. What is the sum of the cubical contents of all the bed-rooms assigned to the boarders in the largest boarding-house? and how many boys sleep in these rooms?—75,660 feet; 66 boys sleep in these rooms. There is also an open passage, and large lobby adjoining, and ventilation at the highest point of the roof.

17. Has every boy a separate bed?—Yes.

18. What are the hours of going to bed and getting up?—Bedtime, 9, little boys, 10, bigger. Getting up time, chapel, 7 in summer, 7.30 a.m. in winter.

19. How is discipline maintained in the bed-rooms?—By Masters and Præpostors.

20. Are there separate rooms for study; if so, to how many boys is one room allotted?—Head Master's house, the cubicles are studies. Second Master's house, separate studies, two in each.

INSTRUCTION AND DISCIPLINE.

21. During how many weeks in the year is the School at work?— Thirty-nine.

22. What, if any thing, are the boys required to know on admission?—To read English perfectly, and write it competently, Statute 24.

23. Is their possession of this knowledge ascertained by examination?—Examined by Head Master.

24. Is the School classified (a) by one leading subject or group of subjects solely; or (b) by one leading subject, &c., chiefly, and other subjects subordinately; or (c) separately for every subject or group of subjects?—By one leading subject (classics); mathematics, French, English, &c., being subordinate.

25. Are boys promoted from class to class (a) by seniority; or (b) by marks gained for work done in the half-year; or (c) by examination at the end of the half-year; or (d) in what other way?—By marks gained for work in half-year, and examination at the end in combination, except that the annual examiner promotes by classics only.

26. Does success in one subject affect the promotion in another subject?—Yes. See answer 24.

27. How many hours a week are the boys in School?—32 in summer, 29 in winter, independently of evening preparation.

28. What proportion of the lessons are learnt (a) in School; (b) out of School under supervision by a Master; (c) out of School not under supervision?—This varies according to the position of a boy in the School. The sixth form learn no lessons under supervision. From the suspension (corresponding to lower fourth) all are learnt under supervision.

29. In learning Latin, Greek, French, and German lessons, are the boys allowed (a) to use translations; or (b) to have assistance from a Master or Tutor; or (c) to have no aid but grammar and dictionary?—Generally they have no aid but grammar and dictionary. In cases of dull or idle boys sometimes they have assistance from a Master or Tutor.

30. Are Latin, Greek, French, and German exercises done (a) in

prose; (*b*) in verse?—Latin and Greek in both prose and verse, French and German only in prose.

31. Are such exercises, if any, (*a*) short sentences taken from exercise-books; (*b*) continuous pieces for translation; (*c*) original composition?—According to the attainments and position of the boys. Short sentences taken from exercise-books from the fourth form downwards; continuous pieces for translation, fifth and sixth. Original composition is rare.

32. Are examples in arithmetic or mathematics (*a*) taken from text books; (*b*) dictated orally by the master; (*c*) set in writing?—All these ways.

33. Are the boys taught natural history, physics, or chemistry (*a*) by text-books; (*b*) by oral lectures; (*c*) with specimen objects and experiments shown by the master or lecturer; (*d*) with specimen objects handled and experiments worked by the boys themselves?—None at present. Classes that have existed for these purposes have been discontinued.

34. Are the following subjects taught, and in what way: (*a*) geometrical drawing; (*b*) perspective; (*c*) freehand drawing from the flat; (*d*) freehand drawing from models; (*e*) colouring?—(*a*) Geometrical drawing not at present.

(*b*) Perspective
(*c*) Freehand from the flat
(*d*) Freehand from models
(*e*) Colouring
} to some boys.

35. Is the theory or practice of music taught?—The practice of music is taught to the choir and to some other boys.

36. How often is the School examined?—Thrice a year, at the close of every term.

37. By what examiners? and how are they appointed?—Twice by the Masters, once by the Masters and an Examiner conjointly appointed by the Governors on the nomination of All Souls' College, Oxford. The Examiner examines the sixth by paper and *vivâ voce*, the rest of the School only *vivâ voce*.

38. In what subjects?—The Masters examine in classics, mathematics, French, &c.; the Examiner only in classics, Statute 37.

39. What system of rewards and prizes is in use in the School?—

Prizes are given to the heads of the respective forms for composition in Greek, Latin, French, and English, for knowledge of Scripture, grammar, &c., &c., and for general merit. Exhibitions are competed for by boys about to leave the School.

40. Is it part of the system to modify the course of the School in the case of boys (a) who show a particular aptitude for certain studies; (b) who are intended by their parents for certain lines of life; (c) who after trial appear specially disqualified for any part of the School work? If so, how is it done?—This system is carried out as far as practicable, by suiting the lessons to the boys' requirements.

41. Is the ordinary School instruction sufficient, without supplementary aid, to prepare a boy of good ability for success in the competitive examinations for Scholarships at the Universities, and for the Civil, Military, and East India Services?—Sufficient for scholarships at the Universities, for the line, and probably for the other services; but for the last three boys generally take special training for a year or so.

42. Is the Head Master supreme over the instruction, or who can interfere with him?—The Head Master is supreme.

43. Is the School connected with any, and if so, with what religious denomination?—With the Established Church, Statutes 1 and 15, which are also original Statutes. See Statute 26, original.

44. What provisions are made for religious instruction?—Scripture lessons on Sunday and Monday mornings before breakfast. A chapter is read in chapel before breakfast, and is the subject of examination in the respective forms after breakfast. Before confirmation there is special instruction to the candidates for about a month.

45. (a) Is the Head Master responsible for the religious instruction? (b) Is any other Master or person?—The Head Master is responsible. Each Master gives such instruction to his own form, and to his boarders if he have any.

46. Does the school-work begin and end with prayers?—The school-work begins and ends with prayers.

47. What prayers are used?—In chapel a selection from the daily service is used. In School one Church prayer is used, and another provided by the Head Master.

48. Are all boys necessarily present at prayers?—Yes.

49. In case of boys whose parents wish them to be confirmed, who is responsible for preparing the boys?—The Head Master.

50. Are there any lessons on Sundays? and how is the day observed?—Lessons on Sundays before breakfast, and in the evening lessons prepared for the next day. The School goes to the parish church in the morning, and to the school-chapel in the afternoon.

51. What are the regulations about attendance on Divine worship on Sunday?—All the School attend at the parish church and school-chapel, Statute 15. Some few attend a district church where their parents attend.

52. Is the Head Master supreme over the discipline? or, if not, who can interfere with him?—He is supreme as regards the ordinary punishments.

53. What punishments are in use? and for what offences are they inflicted?—Lines repeated and written and confinement in School with a Master from 4 to 5 p.m. for bad lessons and ordinary offences. Caning for wilful idleness, lying, &c., &c. Fines for throwing stones and wilful mischief. Flogging with a birch for persistent lying and other moral offences.

54. If corporal punishment is in use, is it inflicted publicly or privately?—Privately; the Head and Second Masters both cane; no other Masters.

55. What punishments, if any, can be inflicted by the Head Master only?—Flogging.

56. What punishments, if any, can be inflicted by the under masters, either with or without reporting to the Head Master or others?—Lines and confinement for an hour without reporting. Fines, by reporting.

57. Are there any monitors or præpostors empowered to aid in maintaining discipline?—Yes.

58. If there are, by whom, and how, are they appointed?—By the Head Master, out of the sixth form. Boys who have been confirmed and undertake personally such duties.

59. What punishments, if any, can they inflict?—Lines and canings.

60. Can they inflict such punishments without reporting to the

Head Master or others?—The boy punished has the power always of appealing against the punishment to the Head Master.

61. Have they any other powers, *e.g.*, that of fagging?—Fagging at cricket and fives, and study fagging where studies exist.

62. Are they required to report any serious evil that they may observe among their schoolfellows?—Yes.

63. Do you believe that they would?—Yes, if they could not stop it. They have done so.

64. Is there any rule that the boys should never be out of the presence of some Master or other?—No.

65. Have the boys access to any School library?—Yes.

66. Under what conditions?—To receive books, but not to sit in the library till they are in the sixth form.

PLAYGROUNDS AND RECREATION.

67. Is there a playground attached to the School?—Yes.
68. If so, is it open to all the boys to use?—Yes.
69. How large is it?—About 12 acres, besides a gravel playground.
70. How far is it from the School?—Adjoining.
71. Have the boys any, and what, covered place for play in wet weather?—No.
72. How many hours a week are allowed for play?—19 hours in mid-winter, 31 in summer, sometimes an extra half-holiday.
73. What are the usual games or other bodily exercises?—Cricket, football, fives, occasionally gymnastics, and a little boating.
74. Is there any rule that a Master should be always present?—No.
75. Do any of the Masters join in the games?—Yes, generally.
76. Is there a gymnasium?—Only a temporary open one.
77. Is drilling, or are any athletic exercises taught as a part of the School system?—No, it has been tried and discontinued.
78. Are there any School bounds beyond the School precincts, or are the boys allowed to walk in the country at their own discretion?—The sixth form have no bounds. The bounds for other boys vary according to their forms. All except præpostors and day-boys answer calls.

Playgrounds and Recreation.

General Questions.

General Questions.

79. What subjects of instruction do you believe to be best fitted for the education of the majority of your scholars?—Classics in combination with mathematics, French, English, and German.

80. What subjects of instruction do you believe to be preferred by the parents?—The above-mentioned.

81. What difficulties, if any, do you find in the discharge of your duty?—In education (*a*) scholarships given with a decided preference to foundationers; (*b*) no School exhibitions provided by the foundation; (*c*) low and varying qualification standard for scholarships; (*d*) little encouragement given to mathematics and other studies. In discipline, day-boys not sufficiently under control of Head Master; they should be in the same position as boarders as regards calls, evening school, &c.

82. Would it, in your opinion, be an advantage or otherwise if your School were examined annually, and publicly reported on by independent Examiners?—It is so examined annually.

83. If such Examiners are desirable, how should they be appointed?—I see no cause for altering our present system of appointment by the Governors on the nomination of All Souls' College[1]. We ought always to have an additional Examiner in mathematics and in modern languages.

84. Is it, in your judgment, possible or expedient to give boys at school a direct preparation for the particular occupations for which they may be intended by their parents?—We should require a separate Master to much smaller classes, and I doubt the possibility or expediency.

I, being the Head Master of the above-named School, hereby certify that the foregoing statements are correct.

(Signed)   J. I. WELLDON, D.C.L.,
Master of Tonbridge School.

June 12th, 1865.

[1] I think it should be a *sine quâ non* that such examiner should have taken a *first* class in moderations.

LIST OF DISTINCTIONS

GAINED AT THE UNIVERSITIES, CIVIL SERVICE EXAMINATIONS, ETC., SINCE 1854[1].

1854. 2nd Class Class. Tripos, Cambridge, G. M. Smith, Scholar of Caius College.
2nd Class Class. Tripos, Cambridge, J. H. K. Ward, Scholar of Trinity College.
Woolwich Artillery, P. M. Guille.

1855. 1st Class Moderations, Oxford, A. P. Howell, Scholar of Trinity.
1st Class Moderations, Oxford, W. R. Morfill, Scholar of Oriel.
Open Fellowship, St. John's College, Oxford, A. P. Howell.
2nd Class History, Wadham College, Oxford, H. J. Bigsby.
Open Scholarship, Oriel College, Oxford, R. G. Penny.
Provis. Commis., Woolwich, H. C. Seddon.
1st at Haileybury, final examination, and formerly Scholar of Trinity College, Cambridge, and Bell University Scholar, M. Melvill.

1856. 2nd Class Lit. Human., Oxford, A. P. Howell.
2nd at Haileybury, final examination; prizes, Hindustani, Classics, Persian, H. Burra.

1857. 2nd Class Mathematics, Moderations, Oxford, T. E. Binney (Brazenose).
Open Scholarship, University College, Oxford, A. R. Pryor.
13th Wrangler, Cambridge, L. Ewbank (Clare Hall).
17th Sen. Opt., Cambridge, H. B. Stevens (Emmanuel).
Woolwich Engineers, H. C. Seddon.
7th India Civil Service examination, A. P. Howell.

1858. 2nd Class Moderations, Oxford, R. G. Penny (Oriel).
Open Scholarship, University College, Oxford, H. St. J. Reade.

[1] I have not been able to go any farther back than this date, as there has been no regular record kept of the Distinctions, and for the same reason I trust that any one whose name I may have inadvertently omitted will forgive me, and also kindly let me know.—S. R.

Distinctions gained at the Universities, &c.

Open Scholarship, Wadham College, Oxford, S. O. B. Ridsdale.
1st Class Phys. Sciences, Cambridge, J. Nottidge (Emmanuel).
18th Sen. Opt., Cambridge, P. G. Skipworth (Emmanuel).
14th Engineer and sword at Addiscombe, Harrison.

1859. 2nd Class Moderations, Oxford, J. Burra (University).
Demyship, Magdalen College, Oxford, R. H. Burrows.
2nd Class Phys. Sciences, Oxford, J. Flower (Exeter).
2nd Class Class. Tripos, Cambridge, B. H. Alford (Trinity).
Open Scholarship, Caius College, Cambridge, E. A. Brown.
Open Scholarship, Pembroke College, Cambridge, C. S. Isaacson.
Port Latin Scholarship, St. John's College, Cambridge, T. T. Falkner.

1860. 1st Class Moderations, Oxford, H. St. J. Reade (University).
2nd Class Moderations, Oxford, S. O. B. Ridsdale (Wadham).
2nd Class Moderations, Oxford, A. F. Nussey (Exeter).
Open Scholarship, Trinity College, Oxford, H. E. P. Platt.
4 College Scholarships.

1861. 1st Class Moderations, Oxford, R. H. Burrows (Magdalen).
1st Class Nat. Science, Oxford, A. B. Shepherd (Brazenose).
Open Scholarship, Brazenose College, Oxford, H. F. O'Hanlon.
Open Scholarship, Christ's College, Cambridge, A. Simpson.
21st in Indian Civil Service examination, S. O. B. Ridsdale.
2 College Scholarships.

1862. 2nd Class Lit. Human., Oxford, H. St. J. Reade (University).
1st Class Moderations, Oxford, H. E. P. Platt (Trinity).
2nd Class Moderations, Oxford, T. W. Greene.
2nd Class Class. Tripos, Cambridge, S. Greatheed (Corpus).
2nd Class Class. Tripos, Cambridge, H. Woodward (Trinity).
2 Provis. Commis., Woolwich, Godson and Clark.

1863. 1st Class Moderations, Oxford, H. F. O'Hanlon (Brazenose).
2nd Class History, Oxford, W. E. McGill (Pembroke).
Math. Lecturer, Clare College, Cambridge, L. Ewbank.
11th Wrangler, Cambridge, C. S. Isaacson (Clare Hall).
1st Class Tripos, Cambridge, T. T. Falkner St. John's).
2nd Class Class. Tripos, Cambridge, E. A. Brown (Caius).
2nd Class Class. Tripos, Cambridge, H. T. McGill (Christ's).

Open Scholarship Trinity, College, Cambridge, J. Greatheed. *Distinctions gained at the Universities, &c.*
Open Scholarship, Christ's College, Cambridge, E. T. Nixon.
1st Class Honours, Inns of Court examination, W. C. Druce.
Woolwich Engineers, T. B. Lindsell.

1864. 1st Class Lit. Human., Oxford, H. E. P. Platt (Trinity).
2nd Class History, Oxford, T. W. Greene (Magdalen).
2nd Class Moderations, Oxford, F. O. Ward (Wadham).
2nd Class Moderations, Oxford, T. F. Burra (University).
2nd Class Class. Tripos, Cambridge, J. Greatheed (Trinity).
Open Scholarship, Catherine's College, Cambridge, F. L. Salusbury.
Warneford Scholarship (Medical), King's College, London, A. McGill.
1st in Law examination, A. Smallpiece.

1865. Open Scholarship, Wadham College, Oxford, W. O. Hughes-Hughes.
1st Class Lit. Human., H. F. O'Hanlon (Brazenose).
1st Class Class. Tripos, Cambridge, A. Simpson (Christ's).
Open Scholarship, Christ's College, Cambridge, A. Nixon.
Warneford Scholarship (Medical), King's College, London, W. B. Whitmore.
Leathes' Prize, King's College, London, G. Milles.

1866. Open Scholarship, Corpus College, Oxford, W. H. B. Lindsell.
Open Scholarship, Exeter College, Oxford, W. G. Walker.
Open Scholarship, Exeter College, Oxford, L. T. Lochée.
Open Scholarship, St. John's College, Cambridge, E. Saxton.
Open Scholarship, Clare College, Cambridge, W. d'A. Barnard.
Open Fellowship, Lincoln College, Oxford, H. F. O'Hanlon.
Indian Civil Service, M. Reade and A. Peet.

1867. Open Scholarship, Trinity College, Oxford, E. B. Nicholson.
Open Scholarship, Brazenose College, Oxford, A. W. D. Campbell.
Open Fellowship, Lincoln College, Oxford, H. E. P. Platt.
Indian Civil Service, A. W. D. Campbell and A. Unwin.

1868. *Proxime accessit* for Balliol College Scholarship, Oxford, F. W. Hughes-Hughes.

Distinctions tions gained at the Universities, &c.

Scholarship, Worcester College, Oxford, Morgan.
2nd Class Moderations, Oxford, W. H. B. Lindsell (Corpus).
2nd Class Class. Tripos, Cambridge, F. L. Salusbury (Catherine's).

1869. Open Scholarship, Corpus College, Oxford, F. W. Hughes-Hughes.
1st Class Moderations, Oxford, E. B. Nicholson (Trinity).
2nd Class Moderations, Oxford, W. G. Walker (Exeter).
2nd Class Moderations, Oxford, L. T. Lochée (Exeter).
Open Exhibition, St. John's College, Cambridge, S. Allnutt.
Open Scholarship, Catherine's College, Cambridge, F. Harding.

SPEECHES
SPOKEN ON SKINNERS' DAY

PROBABLY BETWEEN 1790 AND 1800.

GARDNER.

ROUSE, please, your godship—there's no such mighty harm in't,
   Don't go to sleep, I tell you tisn't a sarmint;
Open your eyes, I'm only speaking verses,
Just as Betts, the bellman, oft rehearses,
When on old New Year's night he gives you warning
Of what's o'clock, and also how's the morning.
Oh could I but boast his soft melodious tongue,
The shrillness of his pipe and strength of lung,
I'd rouse you all with most sonorous numbers,
Not Betts himself should better break your slumbers;
But ah! his oratorical grace and powers
Good mistresses and masters are not ours.
So in my own dull strain I still must creep,
Sleepless myself, to give my hearers sleep.
Be then this congregation o'er so drowsy,
Brother, thus far I've said, and you must now say,
Or else, our Master, there he sits, will rouse ye.

SLATTER.

Indeed, good ladies, ours are sad disasters,
Task upon task impos'd by our taskmasters.

In short, it is the old Egyptian law,
Brick must be made, no matter for the straw.
Bring, says the monarch, bring your tale of rhyme,
In certain measure, at a certain time.
Lord help us, boys! for nothing can dispense
With tasks once set, we beg in vain for sense;
No inspiration, no poetic itch,
Yet rhyme we must, or woe betides the breech,
Say what we will, we must go thro' our part,
Else, ladies, faith, you don't know how we smart.
Ladies, you're kind, to you I'll make my suit,
Pray speak, and don't be too shamefac'd to do't;
Will any one of you, I ask, dispute?
Here, ma'am, my place I'm willing to resign,
Try for a frolick, for I'm sure you'll shine.
Let not your suppliant here thus vainly sue.
I see you smile. Will you? or you? or you?
I'll hand you in; come, come, you'll do't with ease,
There's something in your manners that must please;
The noblest heights of eloquence you'll reach,
For you have naturally the gift of speech,
No pauses, hums, or hahs, but all facility,
All sweetness, grace, and then such volubility.

GARDNER.

Spare we our jokes, he'll make us eat our words,
For beaux have something sharp—that is, their swords.
No, if I trust to them my hopes are undone,
I'll try some gentleman just come from London.
There oratory is still in great request,
And he most votes obtains who speaks the best.
There it avails a man in tropes to hector,
For voice and action get the Sunday lecture.
Stretch out your arms, make faces, hollow loud,
Then build a chapel, and you'll have a crowd.
Oh, the fine man! All feel a satisfaction,
And well they may, for he has voice and action.

Old women sob, grave gemmen cry, "How great!"
And shillings drop by wholesale in the plate.
There's eloquence most truly apostolical,
Compar'd to which old Tully's you may folly call;
Nor in the church alone great speakers bawl;
At vestries, wardmotes, and coachmakers' hall,
'Tis oratory gives weight from the churchwarden
To Mr. Sheridan and Lord George Gordon;
From Dr. Jebb's[1] and Fox's flowing strain
To spouting Benedicts in Foster Lane.
All in this age must figure in debate,
Quite from St. James's down to Billings-gate.
Does any wish to talk and breathe defiance
Where patriots meet in quintuple alliance?
First he applies to Mr. Sheridan,
A sage who holds that spouting maketh man.
Thus arm'd complete by rhetoric prelections,
He hurls at ministers his keen reflections,
Becomes a mighty reformation stirrer,
And vows to cut off every rotten borough;
Slap dash he goes to work, and hap what will,
Cuts rotten boroughs like a rotten apple.
What though his own affairs all run to ruin,
'Tis all to save his country from undoing:
Counter and counting-house forgot, the nation,
The House of Commons, calls for reformation;
His voice, his all, he gives to such a cause,
Whilst fat Clare Market butchers belch applause.

SLATTER.

You mean to say, if any gentleman
Here present has adopted such a plan
Here he may come and exercise his skill,
So we can shirk the task, succeed who will,

---

[1] Jebb, the father of the late Bishop of Limerick; he was, like Sheridan's father, a Professor of Elocution.

Let Tunbridge hear those strokes that charm'd the city.
Suppose a moment this is a committee,
And you a delegate, now spout away
On Liberty; the boys shall shout "Huzza!"
And learn to claim as rights each holiday.

GARDNER.

In vain again we ask—there's no assistance,
Your City orator still keeps his distance,
He feels no pity for a young beginner,
Or does not choose to speak just after dinner.
Well, I've another plan, and let me urge ye
To seek at length the benefit of clergy.

SLATTER.

The clergy! Shish, our master's of the cloth,
And if you touch the clergy will be wrath;
Should you provoke him you'll come off but shabbily,
Think of old Horace and his "*genus irritabile.*"

GARDNER.

I know and feel the reverence justly due,
I only sport a harmless joke, no more do you.
Fear not, "*Licentia sumpta erit decenter,
Adde quod Clerici satis jam implentur
In bonam partem capient,*" never fear it,
Rich was the turbot, nectar was the claret,
And things so good as pie, pudding, do more
Than you may think to put them in good humour.
We should have made our verses more refined,
If we had spoke before their worships dined;
Fine style, fine verse, fine oratoric roaring,
So very fine they'd set you all a-snoring.

SLATTER.

Well, but the gemmen come to share the treat,
'Twas this day's duty not to preach, but eat.

You urge them double duty to endure,
Too much like me—they like a sinecure.
A time for all things; now discourse there's good in,
And now you'll find it in a good plum pudding.
Now you may fast, and now find some relief
In crumbs of comfort from a slice of beef.
Grace they have said, and 'tis enough to say,
Except indeed in hospitable way;
As, pray sir, shall I beg that wing of chicken?
These ducks and peas are mighty pretty picking.
Will you be kind enough to send a slice
Of ham? Indeed, the flavour's very nice;
Sir, shall I ask another plate of fish?
Stop, John, I have not done with that fine dish.
Step to that gentleman who sits so nigh,
And beg another cut of gooseberry-pie.
Here—where's the fellow gone? a larger glass!
Or send the butler for the sparrow-grass.
Sir, to your health! Sir, give me leave to pledge ye?
With all my heart! I hope I do not wedge ye,
I like good elbow-room, good room to work;
Nothing like elbow-room for knife and fork.
Dear sir, I thank ye, I'm afraid I slave ye,
If not, I'll beg one spoonful more of gravy.

GARDNER.

Hush! or you'll soon be made to cry *peccavi*,
If you run on so, some folks will be cross,
They think already that you've too much sauce.
You'll feast till we are sick, the torrent stem,
For tho' you talk so fast, 'tis *nil ad rem*.
They'll not assist you, so leave off requesting,
For while you jest they're busy in digesting—
A work of long internal operation
To do it thoroughly,—so no molestation.
Adieu, then, sirs, and now below the bar
I turn my eyes; Lord! how the good folks stare,

I'm sure, you're all good-natured by your looks;
Aye, marry, are you, tho' not read in books?
You, sir, in brown, pray lay aside your quid,
And lend a hand and tongue this work to rid.
Come, don't be bashful. What, you're for withdrawing!
Now you begin. Oh! no—you're only chawing.
'Tis my opinion though, you're not so shy
You'll talk enough about it by and by.
Aye, aye, I knows as how you argufy,
Can in the Constitution spy each flaw,
Condemn Lord North, at will lay down the law.
I call this speaking. Do you call it jaw?
You give it a too modest appellation,
Yes, sir, you undervalue your oration.
Call it whate'er you will, the truth t' impart ye,
I wish some great ones had been half so hearty.
Had men of Kent their own oak navies led,
The Dons, Mynheers, and Monsieurs, would have bled.
Yes, yes; ye would have told another story,
Spoke to the purpose, and retriev'd our glory;
Spoke to the purpose, and, egad! been at 'em,
Like British tars, last war, set on by Chatham[1].

SLATTER.

Spoke to the purpose, and I wish you'd speak so,
And not your flimsy verses spin on eke so.

GARDNER.

If you're for politics, so far agreed;
I'll be in Opposition, so proceed.
What think you of the Peace[2]?

SLATTER.

I like it not.

---

[1] The great war of Lord Chatham, of which Rolfe's Quebec (1759) was one of the chief instances.

[2] 1782, after Rodney's victory.

GARDNER.

Why so? Tho' something lost, yet something got;
The fur-trade gone [1], you'll say, concerns the Skinners,
But then you get rare turbot for your dinners.
So to express the idea without pomposity,
I think there seems a perfect reciprocity.

SLATTER.

Aye, but our honour!

GARDNER.

Honour, I can tell ye,
Will ne'er like turbot fill a body's belly.
Can honour pay your debts? Ask Dr. Price!
We're sick to death; he'll prove it in a trice;
And so nurse Shelburne [2], pitying our disaster,
Clapt on Britannia's wounds a healing plaister.

SLATTER.

Deuce take the nurse—unless you're very dull, sir,
You'll find an ill-cured sore becomes an ulcer.
'Twas patchwork—so the botcher mends my breeches,
No sooner stitch'd but out fly all the stitches.
Succeeding botchers stitch by turns and curse,
And my poor galligaskins still grow worse.
I wish your botchers (tho' it mayn't be civil)
In their own Hell,—or even at the Devil!

GARDNER.

I see you're rather prone to be satyric,
We'll grant Britannia's doctor an empyric.
But what have I to do with this or you, pray?
"*Id nihil est nos, quod nos est supra.*"
As to all party wrangling I disown 'em;
I like the Peace, for Peace "*per se est bonum.*"

[1] At the close of the American war many hunting-grounds which the Hudson's Bay Company claimed were then handed over to America.

[2] Lord Shelburne's administration, which was any thing but glorious for England.

I take the hint, and since our country's swords
Are sheath'd, suppose we end this war.
The House agree—not one dissentient voice
And *inter nos*—they've reason to rejoice.
We, after all—I hope it no disgrace is—
Must, like the Shelburne party, quit our places.

SLATTER.

With all my heart, we drop our opposition,
And make for once an honest coalition.

GARDNER.

Hah, hah ! sly fox, I see you ken your wa',
Go out awhile, come in with fresh eclat.
Yes, by next year we hope to improve our cause,
And closely following our preceptor's laws,
To earn what now your candour gives, applause.

COLLOQUIUM INTER ROBERT MITFORD AND STEPHEN WOODGATE, MAY 9, 1799.

M. I cannot say one syllable !
W. Hey-day !
 The company all met, and you not say !
M. I could say once ; but now, through fear, I fail ;
 My nerves all tremble, and my face grows pale.
W. What ! I suppose the assembly here abashes ?
M. O yes ! my bloodless cheeks are white as ashes.
W. True, aye, I see it, clear as the full moon,
 Some rouge and drops there—or the boy will swoon ;
 Your ghastly, ghost-like visage folks must shock,
 White as vermilion, or a Turkey cock.
M. The ladies smile though ; then my fears are over,
 My courage and my colour I recover.

But as for rouge—for others keep your satire,
No colours here but simple tints of nature.
W. No, but they say (I scarcely think it true)
That Bond-street beaux add paint to nature's hue.
M. Paint! what! men paint?
W. Why, yes.
M. The devil they do!
What colour? Is it then Circassian bloom[1],
Whose hues feign liveliness, whose scents perfume?
W. The colour, you'll not guess, I'll lay a crown.
M. Black?
W. No.
M. Blue?
W. No.
M. What then?
W. Why, brown.
M. Brown of all colours! Why? I ask again?
W. I guess, because they wish to look like men.
So delicate and lily-white their cheeks,
The soft complexion less than man bespeaks.
No bearded bravoes they! nor bluff, nor brawny!
But painted well, they look a little tawny.
The wish is to appear as if they'd been at sea,
Drank flip and grog, though they drink only tea!
M. Tea only! pardon me, that's not your sort;
Though not at sea, egad, they're deep in port;—
Port admirals they are.
W. With cheeks so sallow
If admirals they are, tis of the yellow.
Checked shirts they wear too, and the neckcloths blue.
M. Or blue or brown—the colours are not true;
A man of Kent, I'll lay a brace of dollars,
Would with his finger make them strike their colours.

---

[1] Compare, for instance, Rowland's Kalydor of the present day.

W. O shame on such! yet such you often meet,
Sauntering and strutting in St. James's-street:
Yellow their lilies are, and as for roses,
None, if we credit either eyes or noses.
Alas! no flowrets, sweet and balmy, blow
Along Fop's-alley or in Rotten-row:
So their sweet hues and odours all are got,
Not from the garden, but the gallipot.

M. If we may credit what is said in rumours,
Much of their money goes to the perfumers;
And all to please the ladies!

W.   No, no, brother,
'Tis all to please themselves, or one another.

M. Proud, empty, nauseous, and malignant vermin!
To scorn, and hate, and shun them, I determine.
I'd rather vegetate and be a hop,
Than cumber earth, a good-for-nothing fop.
Grant I may store my mind, and teach my heart
To act through life an useful, manly part!

W. Give me your hand—in this we're both agreed;
Oh, could our verse exterminate the breed!
Perpetual war with puppies would I wage,
The pest, the bane, the nuisance of the age.
Pity such nothings fashion should approve;
Oh, may they never gain the ladies' love!

M. The ladies cannot love whom they despise,
But with their fans repulse, as buzzing flies.
So shift the scene, and bring forth men of merit,
Who act with virtue, dignity, and spirit.
What think you now of Nelson?

W. Past all praise!
A trophy to his glory who can raise?

M. A grateful nation: his the glory be
Of valour sanctified by piety:
A noble, virtuous, singular example,
In times when men on sacred matters trample.

W. How must the beaux and sophs, so pert and flighty,
Triflers, who dare with sneers insult the Almighty,
Shrink when they hear the man whom Britain boasts
Ascribe all glory to the Lord of Hosts [1].
M. How I could laugh, or rather (I think) cry,
O'er impious nonsense dubbed philosophy!
Of which, it seems, the principle and plan
Makes all mankind as wretched as it can.
W. May never such infect the British youth,
Still may they feed their minds with wholesome truth;
Still, still revere (whate'er from fools may spring)
Their God, their laws, their liberty, and king!
M. Well prayed! and to the prayer, I say, Amen,
And so will say nine Britons out of ten.
W. But then, whate'er we wish, whate'er we say,
I fear we must not only pray, but pay.
What think you of the taxes?
M. Now, you touch
A string that jars and vibrates pretty much;
Most men have feeling; prithee, do not shock it.
W. True; and their feeling's chiefly in their pocket.
M. I wish you had not on this subject spoke;
The income-tax, believe me, is no joke.
Nobody laughs—oh, no! there's not a single grin!
No, says old Gripus, let them laugh that win.
W. Old Gripus was a sly, old, mumping codger,
As Crœsus rich, but—still he was a dodger.
No carriages kept he, no liveried slave;
He'd walk to Scotland, could he sixpence save.
His only grief, whate'er the way or weather,
To wet his thread-bare coat, or wear shoe-leather.
Thus snug, he saved his farthings and his pence,
And laughed at men who rode, as void of sense.
Let Pitt lay taxes triple or quadruple,
He 'scaped them all without a qualm or scruple.

---

[1] This alludes to the commencement of Nelson's Despatch from the Nile, "Almighty God has blessed His Majesty's arms with a great victory," &c.

    Pitt, of the Fox got scent (for much he stunk,
    As to his earth the crafty varlet slunk),
    And caught him in a gin; in vain he locks
    His cash and paper in his strongest box.
    Pitt's an overmatch for Master Fox.
    The hunters follow, Reynard cannot slink'em,
    Forced to lug out the tenth of all his income.

M. Rare sport and fair! as far as I can see;
    Let him be skinned—for many a flint skinned he.
    Out with his hoard! a dunghill should be spread
    To make the blossoms flourish in the mead;
    The putrid mass well scattered shall produce
    Flowers for delight, and corn and hay for use.

W. So far, so well! the tax is good and fit
    For misers, since the biter should be bit;
    But to tax genius joined with industry
    More than the lazy, is to kill the bee
    And spare the drone.

M. Well, I declare, I'm willing
    To pay a tenth out of my weekly shilling,
    After deductions made for necessaries,
    Nuts, apples, custards, and vagaries.
    For I'm no Gripus; if I have a tart,
    My school-fellows are welcome to a part,
    My heart is open and my pocket too.
    To serve my country, what would I not do?

W. To serve our country! 'tis a noble aim,
    I praise your ardour and I feel the same.
    But how? for money? little is our lot,
    And many calls we have for what we've got.
    Tops, hoops, bats, balls, dumps, marbles, gingerbread,
    And a few whims we take into our head,
    Leave little for our country—rather nil;
    So Mr. Pitt, accept of our good-will.

M. Our income small, and great the expenditure,
    Yet will I give a penny to the poor;

For better far I deem it to bestow
A pittance to alleviate human woe;
Than lavish millions in the laurelled plain,
Where conquest struts with carnage in his train.
"Nor yet doth glory, tho' her port be bold,
Her aspect radiant and her tresses gold,
Guide through the walks of death alone her car,
Attendant only on the pomp of war."
She has, I hope, in store, a brilliant crown
For arts of peace; for works of love, renown.
A niche in fame's high temple for the good,
Such as Sir Thomas Smythe, Sir Andrew Judde,
And all his sons, who still from year to year,
Their bounty to dispense, assemble here.
And still unchecked by taxes on their store,
Diminish not, but give the needy more.
With winter garments clothe, supply with bread,
And smooth the pillow for the hoary head.

W. Such deeds surpass all human praise; yet I,
Who love, like you, a finger in a pie,
Lament the absence of one Mr. Birch [1]
(Pity that he should leave us in the lurch);
Birch that whips cream, I mean,—not boys that twitches
With its confounded lacerating switches.
No feast!

M.   O yes! a feast of charity!
And doing good! the finest luxury!
Can venison, turtle, claret, port afford
Such joy as furnishing the poor man's board?
The hungry with good things are filled, and pray
What harm, if rich men empty go away?

W. None; yet you'll wonder not, if boys can't part
Without one longing, lingering look at raspberry tart.
Forgive me if, with finger in my eye,
I mourn the loss of Birch's far-famed pie.

---

[1] Alderman Birch, the famous pastrycook in Cornhill.

      Flow, flow, sweet elegy, in plaintive mood,
        How my mouth waters for the lost repast;
      The gooseberry pie was so extremely good!
        Still on my palate dwells the luscious taste.
M. Aye; but consider 'midst the loss of cheer,
   The public gains a thousand pounds a year.
   No sordid views, illiberal and confined,
   Turned from its generous course our patrons' mind;
   But patriot love, which taught them to forego
   The joys that from convivial pleasures flow,
   To serve their country.
W.   That was nobly done!
   And I applaud, and all my griefs are gone,
   When wars and income-taxes cease; why then
   Perchance we may enjoy a feast again;
   For though we joke, it yet must be confessed,
   There lay the cream and marrow of the jest.
M. Should e'er the ancient hospitable way
   Return with peace, on some auspicious day,
   The room is ready (thanks to one you know,
   The gemmen see it as to church they go);
   A large and lofty room! for feasts and balls,
   (Oft may we dance and shake its massy walls!)
   Sacred to friendship, love, and joy it stands,
   Reared for us by a generous neighbour's hands;
   And oft may friendship, love, and joy unite
   Beneath its roof, to give and take delight.
   And still while beauty views the bands around her
   Let Bacchus crown the cup and hail the Founder.
W. Beneath that roof, you'll give me leave to say,
   To see assemblies happy, blithe, and gay,
   The Founder's bounty amply will repay.
M. Meantime, for other cares our thoughts engage,
   Studious to pore o'er learning's copious page,
   For pleasure palls, unless with business joined,
   Unnerves the body and destroys the mind:
   All noise, all nonsense, and all outside show,
   The manly scholar dwindled to a beau.

W. That character I think we can't adopt,
  Thus having laughed at beaux, both wigged and cropt.
  No, I for my part aim at useful knowledge,
  And wish to shine an honour to my college;
  Hence to the bar or pulpit I aspire,
  And glow with virtuous emulation's fire,
  Still upward soaring with an eagle's ken
  To all that's good and honoured among men.
M. I wish to see (for who would wishes grudge?)
  You made a bishop, and myself a judge.
  A periwig might then become our phizzes,
  Revered and honoured, neither beaux nor quizzes;
  You leaning on the cushion of a stall,
  I on the bench in Westminster's famed hall.
W. Upon my word! you seem a lad of spirit,
  But ere we gain, let's strive the prize to merit:
  Success no mortal can command, but know
  We may command what kings can ne'er bestow,
  With Heaven's blessings, and our own endeavour,
  We may be learned and honest, good and clever.
  Then may we happy and respected be,
  In the mild shades of deep obscurity,
  At Tudely-cum-Capel, or at Pembury.
M. The first great object, wish and care, I find
  Is to adorn and cultivate the mind;
  Then to parental care what obligation,
  That gives us here a liberal education!
  Oh may we prize the gift, the means improve,
  And gain our country's and our parents' love.
W. Nor of our patrons here, who patient sit,
  To hear the ramblings of a schoolboy's wit,
  Unmindful let us be; but while we live,
  Strive the best fruits of gratitude to give,
  By doing honour to the place revered,
  Where smiles like theirs our infant virtues reared.
M. Such be our aim! and now, good gentlemen,
  Vouchsafe to grant a garland and a pen.

www.ingramcontent.com/pod-product-compliance
Lightning Source LLC
Chambersburg PA
CBHW032001230426
43672CB00010B/2229